Y0-CDL-059

Words for Students of English

Vocabulary Series Editors
Holly Deemer Rogerson
Lionel Menasche

WORDS
for Students of English

A Vocabulary Series for ESL

Holly Deemer Rogerson
Gary Esarey
Carol Jasnow
Suzanne T. Hershelman
Dorolyn A. Smith
Carol Moltz
Linda M. Schmandt

Pitt Series in English as a Second Language

Ann Arbor
University of Michigan Press

Reprinted Edition
authorized by the University of Michigan Press
Copyright © by University of Michigan, 1992
Licensed for sale in Korea only
Not for export

Published on July 2003
By Ladder Korea Inc
B-45 COEX World Trade Center
Kangnam-Ku Samsung-Dong Seoul 135-731
Telephone 02-6000-8323   Facsimile 02-6000-8322
Publishing License No : 16-2079, registered on January 13, 2000
Publisher : Don-Gap Choi

All rights reserved. No part of this publication may be reproduced, stored in a
retrieval system, or transmitted in any form or by any means, electronic, mechanical,
photocopying, recording or otherwise, without the prior written permission
of the copyright holder

ISBN : 89-90259-05-3
        89-90259-07-X (Set)

Contents

Foreword

The objective of this series of vocabulary texts for the student of English as a foreign language is to facilitate the learning of approximately 3,000 new base words. Vocabulary learning has long been deemphasized in language teaching, much to the detriment of the students, who have mostly been left to fend for themselves. We thoroughly agree with Muriel Saville-Troike, who states, "Vocabulary knowledge in English is the most important aspect of oral English proficiency for academic achievement" (*TESOL Quarterly*, vol. 18, no. 2, p. 216).

With the present lack of comprehensive vocabulary texts suitable for both classroom use and home study, this series is intended to support teachers in preparing effective vocabulary lessons so that they can meet their students' urgent need for an increased lexicon. We present here a selection of base vocabulary items and some of their derived forms (i.e., the noun, verb, adverb, and adjective of the same stem) together with a series of exercises designed to help students remember the new words and use them in context.

This text has been used in an experimental edition in the English Language Institute, and modifications suggested by its use have been incorporated in the present version.

Christina Bratt Paulston
Director, English Language Institute
University of Pittsburgh

Acknowledgments

A series such as this depends greatly on the cooperation and hard work of numerous people:

Christina Bratt Paulston and Holly Deemer Rogerson originated the idea for the series.

Christina Bratt Paulston provided ongoing support for the series.

Mary Newton Bruder, Carol Jasnow, Christina Bratt Paulston, and Holly Deemer Rogerson developed the first version of the list of approximately 600 words assumed known.

Holly Deemer Rogerson developed the original pool of words from which the 150 topic word lists were chosen. She also organized the word lists and provided general management of the project, including authors' drafts, revisions, editing, illustrations, duplicating, testing, and typing.

Ideas for word lists, format, and exercise types were contributed by Betsy Davis, Gary Esarey, Suzanne T. Hershelman, Carol Jasnow, Carol Moltz, Lionel Menasche, Holly Deemer Rogerson, Dorolyn Smith, and Linda M. Schmandt.

Final revisions of content were done by Lionel Menasche and Holly Deemer Rogerson, with input from classroom testing by Isabel Dillener, Caroline Haessly, Pat Furey, Carol Jasnow, Linda M. Schmandt, Jill Sherman, and Tom Swinscoe.

JoEllen Walker typed several drafts of the manuscript.

Lisa Krizmanich assisted during the testing phase.

Introduction

Volumes 1–6 of *Words for Students of English*, each containing 25 units, present English base words,* with definitions, examples, and exercises. The texts may be used as core texts for vocabulary learning classes or as supplementary texts in reading, speaking, and writing classes. They may also be used for individual study.

Each unit focuses on one topic so that the words being presented can be practiced in meaningful contexts. Some of the new words in each unit are directly related to the topic, while others are less directly connected. Most of the words in a given unit can be used in a variety of contexts.

Volume 1 assumes a knowledge of 600 base words in English. Starting from this point, new words are presented in each unit, with the definitions, examples, and exercises *containing only vocabulary which has been previously learned.* The first units in Volume 1 contain only about ten base words each in order to allow the students to become familiar with the format of the units. After the first units, each unit in Volume 1 contains approximately fifteen base words. In Volume 2, there are approximately fifteen base words in each unit. In Volumes 3 and 4, each unit contains fifteen to twenty base words, and, in Volumes 5 and 6, there are approximately 25 base words per unit. On completion of the series of six volumes, students will have learned approximately 3,000 base words.

Given that Volume 1 assumes a knowledge of 600 base words, the level of Volumes 1 and 2 can be loosely described as beginning, Volumes 3 and 4 as intermediate, and Volumes 5 and 6 as high intermediate or advanced.

---

*"Base" may be defined variously in lexical analysis, but for our present pedagogical purpose it implies any alternant from which other forms are derived. It is frequently impossible to say which form of a word is the most basic.

Selection of Words and Unit Topics

The 600 assumed words upon which Volumes 1–6 are based were chosen by a panel of experienced ESL teachers at the University of Pittsburgh as the group of words which are most typically learned by ESL students during their first two years of middle school or high school ESL classes. The words presented in Volumes 1–6 were selected according to usefulness from a variety of word-frequency lists. The authors and editors added other words to the topics at suitable levels of difficulty.

In many cases students have to learn words with more than one meaning or with meanings that may vary according to context. A decision was made in each such instance as to whether the meaning in the new context was different enough to warrant further definition or similar enough for the students to extrapolate from what they had previously learned. These decisions were based on dictionary definitions and authors' or editors' personal judgments. For example, a word such as *beat* might appear in these contexts: (a) beat the opposing football team, (b) beat a drum, (c) a beat of a heart, (d) beat a person. Contexts (b) and (d) (meaning = strike) were judged close enough to allow extrapolation of meaning from one context to another, but (a) and (c) were thought to require separate definitions.

We have assumed that when a student learns a new vocabulary item, an approximate meaning for the word is assimilated, and that meaning is linked to the context in which the word was first encountered. Then, as the student meets the word in other contexts, the initially learned, approximate meaning is expanded and refined. Hence, many words are not only used several times in the unit in which they first appear, but are also used in later units.

The unit topics were chosen and ordered according to their perceived relevance to the students' lives, that is, their communicative usefulness. Most topics are covered in one unit in each volume, but certain broad topics, for example "School," are repeated twice within the same volume, in which case they are marked (A) or (B). A few topics, such as "Religion" and "Banking," due to the difficulty or abstractness of the words associated with them, are not covered in the first volume. Certain other topics whose words were perceived as tangible and easy, for example, "Telephone" and "Post Office," are completed in the first two volumes.

It should be noted that the repetition of each topic, at times within the same volume and always in at least one subsequent volume, allows for review and recycling of the material learned. Thus, long-term retention of the vocabulary is facilitated.

Format and Suggestions for Teachers

Flexibility in using this vocabulary series has been a prime consideration in planning the format and exercises of the units. Therefore, although suggestions are given in the following paragraphs, it is assumed that teachers in different situations will decide according to their own students' needs whether work should be done in or out of class, orally or in writing, and with or without direct assistance from the teacher. The pace at which classes can proceed through each volume will vary greatly, depending on the students' motivation, study habits, and general workload, as well as the degree of emphasis the teacher wishes to place on productive vocabulary skills.

Each unit in Volumes 1–6 has the same format. The five sections of each unit are as follows.

WORD FORM CHART
DEFINITIONS AND EXAMPLES
INTRODUCTORY EXERCISES
STUDY EXERCISES
FOLLOW-UP

The WORD FORM CHART presents base words and some or all of their related forms, categorized by part of speech. In Volumes 1 and 2, an effort was made to simplify the charts by omitting many derived or related forms which were either not common, or not useful for students at this level, or not easily recognizable from a knowledge of the base form. After Volume 2, more related forms are added because the students can handle more as they progress in learning the language. Decisions on what forms to omit were made by authors and editors on the basis of experience gained during testing of these materials with linguistically heterogeneous classes. Teachers in different educational contexts should consider supplementing the charts according to their own students' needs and their ability to absorb more material. For example, many words could be added by giving antonyms formed from words already given (planned/unplanned, honest/dishonest).

In the NOUNS column of the charts in Volumes 1 and 2 only, nouns which normally or frequently refer to humans are marked by the symbol ⺅. When a noun, as defined in the unit, can be either human or nonhuman, the symbol is in parentheses: (⺅). Gerunds are not included in the charts. Nouns have not been marked "count" and "non-count" because so many nouns function in both ways.

In the VERBS column, irregular past tenses and past participles are in parentheses following the verbs. In cases where more than one past tense or past participle is acceptable, the more regular one is included in the chart. Thus, for example, in the Volume 1, Unit #4 Word Form Chart no irregular forms are listed for *forecast* because the regular form *forecasted* is also currently acceptable.

In the ADJECTIVES column, we have included any present or past participles that appear prenominally as adjectives, as well as any regular adjectives. We have not included in this column nouns which form Noun-Noun modification patterns.

The next section, DEFINITIONS AND EXAMPLES, gives the meanings of the words as well as example sentences which are usually related to the topic of the unit. The form chosen for definition is not always the base form. Other forms are sometimes chosen for greater ease of definition or learning. In all definitions and examples, only previously learned words are used. This applies also within the set of definitions in each unit. Thus, the words in each set of definitions are presented in an order which allows their definition and exemplification using only previously introduced words. Grammatical information is given in the definitions by means of the following conventions: "to" is used before a verb to indicate the verb form, articles are used with nouns whenever possible to indicate that the word is a noun, and parentheses enclose prepositions that may follow a verb. Words with more than one meaning are cross-referenced to definitions in earlier units when new definitions are given. This section, together with the Word Form Chart, can be efficiently handled as work assigned for intensive individual study, followed by discussion in class of questions raised by students. At this point the teacher may also wish to elaborate on certain definitions and give further examples.

Writing explicit definitions of words using the intentionally limited vocabulary available results in some rather broad definitions and others that are limited to certain aspects of the meaning. The deliberate compromise here between precision and generality is designed to make the text fully accessible to students by avoiding the major weakness of many other vocabulary texts: defining new items with words that are themselves unknown to the learner. The easily understood broad definitions, which may take the form of a standard verbal definition, a picture, or a list of examples, are then refined by further exposure to appropriate examples in this unit and series and in the students' later reading. Also, students can usefully refer to a bilingual dictionary in conjunction with studying the example sentences given.

After the Definitions and Examples section, there is a three-tiered system of exercises sequenced to take the student from easy, open-book, fairly controlled exercises through more difficult, less controlled exercises to a final phase with communicative exercises.

The first part of the sequence consists of INTRODUCTORY EXERCISES. These are designed to acquaint the students with the new words in the unit and lead them to an initial understanding of the words by using the Definitions and Examples section. We recommend that these brief and easy exercises be done with books open, orally or in writing, immediately after the teacher's first presentation of the new words.

The next section in each unit, headed STUDY EXERCISES, is a longer and more difficult set of exercises designed to be used by the students for individual study or for oral or written work in class.

The final section is the FOLLOW-UP. This includes a dictation and more open-ended communicative exercises designed to be done after the students have studied the words. The latter may be done orally in class, or teachers may request written answers to selected questions.

Each volume also contains an INDEX listing all the base words presented in that volume. Words in the preceding volumes are given in separate appendices. With each word is listed the volume and unit where it is presented. The 600 initially assumed words are also in an appendix.

An ANSWER KEY at the end of each volume provides answers for all the exercises in the Study Exercises sections, except where a variety of answers is acceptable. Answers are not provided for the Introductory Exercises or the exercises in the Follow-Up so that the teacher can choose to use these exercises for homework or testing purposes if desired.

Production and Recognition

Although a distinction between vocabulary known for recognition and that known for production is often propounded, the actual situation is probably best represented by a continuum stretching from mere recognition to production which is accurate both semantically and syntactically. The exercises in Volumes 1–6 cover the full range of this continuum so that teachers wishing to stress productive vocabulary knowledge will have ample opportunity to give their students feedback on the use of the new words in their speech and writing. However, the goal of many teachers will be to increase their students' recognition vocabularies as rapidly as possible, with the expectation that those words which students meet again frequently in other contexts and have a use for will gradually become part of their productive vocabularies. Teachers with this goal of recognition vocabulary development in mind will wish to proceed more rapidly through the units and deemphasize those exercises requiring productive capabilities, for example, by limiting their corrections to semantic errors, rather than correcting syntactic mistakes as well.

Words for Students of English

Education (A)

Word Form Chart

NOUN	VERB	ADJECTIVE	ADVERB
administration	administer		
administrator		administrative	
advice	advise	advisable	advisably
advisor			
attitude		attitudinal	
cleverness		clever	cleverly
confusion	confuse	confused	confusedly
		confusing	confusingly
equipment	equip	equipped	
fairness		fair	fairly
		unfair	
		intermediate	
knowledge	know	known	
		knowing	knowingly
neatness		neat	neatly
option	opt	optional	optionally
orientation	orient	oriented	
patience		patient	patiently
impatience		impatient	impatiently
record	record	recorded	
		recording	
registration	register	registered	
registrar			
substitute	substitute	substituted	
substitution			
youth		youthful	youthfully

Definitions and Examples

1. **administer** [to manage an office or a school]

   City schools are **administered** by the city government.

   A: Is that your professor?
   B: No. He's an **administrator**.

2. **advise** [to give someone ideas about what to do]

   My professor **advised** me to take chemistry this year.

   A: Did you talk to your **advisor**?
   B: Yes, but she never gives me good **advice**.

3. **attitude** [how you feel about someone or something]

   Success in the university may depend on your **attitude**.

   A: Why don't you like your advisor?
   B: She says I've got a bad **attitude** toward school.

4. **clever** [mentally quick]

   Clever students do not always get good grades.

   A: Why did you only get a "C" on this?
   B: The professor said my idea was **clever**, but my answer wasn't complete.

5. **equipment** [necessary tools]

   The new laboratory is finished, but there is no **equipment** in it yet.

   A: There's nothing in here but tables.
   B: This is the worst **equipped** lab I've ever seen.

6. **fair** [with equal consideration to all]

   A good professor must be **fair** to all students.

   A: Did you talk to your professor?
   B: Yes. I told her that I thought the test was **unfair**.

7. **confuse** [to mistake; to cause someone to be unsure]

   Some lectures are very **confusing**.

   A: Well, do you understand this problem now?
   B: Not really. I'm still a little **confused**.

8. **intermediate** [middle]

> After the beginning course, many students take **intermediate** level mathematics.
>
> A: I think I'll take **intermediate** French.
> B: I think you're ready for the advanced course.

9. **patience** [the ability to stay calm and wait]

> Scientists have to have a lot of **patience**.
>
> A: I'd like to graduate and start making money.
> B: You'll have to be **patient**. It takes a while.

10. **knowledge** [how much you know]

> A university education should increase your **knowledge** of the world.
> The professor's **knowledge** of the history of science was very great.

11. **neat** [clean; carefully arranged]

> The new student had a **neat**, well-dressed appearance.
> She dressed **neatly** for the interview.
> The first thing the interviewer looked for was **neatness**.

12. **optional** [not compulsory]

> Because some courses are **optional**, students have some freedom of choice.
>
> A: Are you taking history this term?
> B: No. It's **optional**, and I'm too busy already.

13. **orientation** [learning about a new environment]

> New students have to attend a week long **orientation** program to learn about life at the university.
>
> A: This place is really confusing.
> B: It takes a while to get **oriented**.

14. **record** [data; information about someone or something]

> **Records** of each student are kept by the school administration.
>
> A: Did the university accept you?
> B: No. They say they can't find any **record** of my application.

15. **youth** [a young person, especially a man; the time of life between childhood and adulthood]

> **Youth** is a time of great hope and excitement.
> The class consisted of three older women and two **youths**.

16. **register** [to enter your name on an official record]

   All students have to **register** before the beginning of the new school year.

   A: Have you **registered** for classes yet?
   B: Not yet. The **registrar's** office was closed.

17. **substitute** [to take or use someone or something in place of another]

   You can **substitute** biology for chemistry, and take chemistry next year.
   Our professor was sick, so a **substitute** came in to teach the class.

Introductory Exercises

A. Match each word with its definition.

   ____ 1. to tell someone what to do
   ____ 2. not compulsory
   ____ 3. the ability to stay calm and wait
   ____ 4. adaptation to a new environment
   ____ 5. a young person
   ____ 6. how much you know
   ____ 7. clean; carefully arranged
   ____ 8. to take someone or something in place of another
   ____ 9. to manage
   ____ 10. to mistake; to cause someone to be unsure

   a. administer
   b. advise
   c. attitude
   d. confuse
   e. equipment
   f. knowledge
   g. neat
   h. optional
   i. orientation
   j. patience
   k. record
   l. register
   m. substitute
   n. youth

B. Answer each question with a word from the word form chart in this unit.

   1. What do you call a person who manages an office?
   2. Whom do you see for help in selecting courses?
   3. What's another word for a "young person"?
   4. What do students have to do before they can take a course?
   5. How would you describe a student who is not sure of what to do or where to go?
   6. What level course do you take before the advanced level?

7. What word describes a course that you do not have to take?
8. What kind of program might help you adapt to a new school?
9. If your regular instructor cannot come today, who might come in his or her place?
10. What word describes a teacher who behaves toward all students with equal consideration?

Study Exercises

C. Write **T** if the sentence is true and **F** if it is false.

——— 1. An advisor may help you choose your courses.

——— 2. Clever people do not have any good attitudes at all.

——— 3. Neatness of clothing can help you in a job interview.

——— 4. An orientation program can help you get to know your university better.

——— 5. Grades are optional at most schools.

——— 6. The easiest courses are at the intermediate level.

——— 7. If you don't register for the course, you probably won't get a grade.

——— 8. Many young people are impatient.

——— 9. School records may be kept on computers.

——— 10. Chemists don't need much equipment.

D. In the blanks, write the appropriate word(s) from the word form chart in this unit.

1. You need a lot of ——————— when you deal with student problems.

2. Your ——————— can help you select the courses you need in order to graduate.

3. The ——————— program was very helpful for new students.

4. The biology lab needed a lot of new ——————— .

5. Interviewers often look for a neat appearance and a

   positive ——————— .

6. She knows everything about physics, but her ——————— of political science is very weak.

7. For new students the campus is very _____ , but in a few weeks you will find your way around easily.

8. I couldn't register. They told me my _____ were lost.

E.   Make sentences with the words.

1. me / my / told / advisor / chemistry / to take

    _____

2. to / of his students / is / that professor / fair / most

    _____

3. English / is / is not / but / optional / physics

    _____

4. confusing / confused / the textbook / is / am / and / I

    _____

5. impatient / she / chemistry / to take / is / intermediate level

    _____

6. the first day / looked / of school / he / neat

    _____

F.   Read the passage and answer the questions that follow.

       The task of being accepted and enrolled in a university begins early for some students, long before they graduate from high school. These students take special courses to prepare for advanced study. They may also take one or more
5 examinations that test how well prepared they are for the university. In the final year of high school, they complete applications and send them, with their student records, to the universities which they hope to attend. Some students may be required to have an interview with representatives of
10 the university. Neatly dressed, and usually very frightened, they are determined to show that they have a good attitude and the ability to succeed.
       When the new students are finally accepted, there may be one more step they have to take before registering for
15 classes and getting to work. Many colleges and universities offer an orientation program for new students. In these programs, the young people get to know the procedures for

registration and student advising, university rules, the use of
the library and all the other major services of the college or
20 university. They also get a chance to meet some of the other
new students, some professors, and some university
administrators.

Beginning a new life in a new place can be very
confusing. The more knowledge students have about the
25 school, the easier it will be for them to adapt to the new
environment.

1. When may some students begin the process of being accepted by a

   college or university? _____

   _____

2. How do these students prepare themselves for advanced study? _____

   _____

3. What things might they send to the university or college which they

   would like to attend? _____

   _____

4. Is an interview compulsory at some universities? _____

   _____

5. What is "orientation?" _____

   _____

6. Who might new students meet at an orientation program? _____

   _____

Follow-up

G. Dictation: Write the sentences that your teacher reads aloud.

   1. _____

   2. _____

   3. _____

4. _____

5. _____

H. Answer the following questions.

Preparing for university in your country:

1. What kinds of knowledge do people need?
2. What records do people need?
3. Whom do they talk to to arrange their programs?
4. What can the advisor help them with?
5. Is the system for entering university fair? Explain.

At the university in your country:

6. Is there an orientation? Describe it.
7. Are any courses optional? Which one(s)?
8. Is the equipment in the science laboratories satisfactory?

I. Explain the process of entering a university in your country.

Transportation (A)

Word Form Chart

NOUN	VERB	ADJECTIVE	ADVERB
angle		angular	
bend	bend (bent, bent)	bent	
caution		cautious	cautiously
connection	connect	connecting	
division	divide	divided	
divider		dividing	
fare			
iron			
jet			
	land		
		main	mainly
motion		motionless	motionlessly
pilot			
politeness		polite	politely
		impolite	impolitely
pull	pull		
steel			
		straight	

Definitions and Examples

1. **jet** [a very fast airplane]

    The military first used **jets**.
    To fly from New York to London, you take a **jet**.

2. **land** [to return to the earth]

>   The jet will **land** in ten minutes.
>   The plane **landed** at the airport.
>   **Landing** the damaged jet was difficult.

3. **fare** [the money you pay for a trip in a taxi, bus, train, etc.]

>   The basic bus **fare** in this city is one dollar.
>
>   Passenger: How much is the **fare** to the airport?
>   Taxi driver: Twelve dollars.

4. **pilot** [the driver of an airplane]

>   My brother is a **pilot** in the air force.
>   The **pilot** of the jet landed the damaged plane safely.

5. **pull** [the opposite of push]

>   The sign on the door said "**PULL**."
>   The man **pulled** the child out of the pool.

6. **divide** [to separate into two or more groups]

>   Six **divided** by two is three.
>   The woman **divided** the food among her children.

7. **main** [the most important]

>   His **main** interest is computers; he spends all his time working
>   with them.
>   The most important street in many American towns is called
>   "**Main** Street."

8. **motion** [the movement]

>   The **motion** of a moving car makes some people feel sick.
>   They pushed the car to put it in **motion**.

9. **cautious** [careful]

>   You should be **cautious** when you cross the street.
>   The sign outside of the construction area said "**CAUTION**."
>   He is a very **cautious** man; he always thinks very carefully before
>   he makes a decision.

10. **straight** [with no change in direction]

>   **Straight** roads are the safest ones.
>   A **straight** line is the shortest distance between two places.

11. **bend** [a change in direction]

We could not see around the **bend** in the road.

12. **bent** [not straight]

The door of my car does not shut easily because it was **bent** in an accident.
My key is **bent** and will not fit into the lock.

13. **iron** [a heavy, silver-white metal which occurs naturally in rocks]

Iron is found in the ground.
This area of the country is rich in **iron**.
Iron is used to make many things.

14. **steel** [a metal made from iron which bends and is used to make cars, buildings, etc.]

Steel is produced from iron in factories.
Steel is heated and bent to form the bodies of cars.

15. **angle** [the corner which is made when two surfaces or straight lines meet]

We measure **angles** in degrees.
The **angles** of the bends in that road make driving on it dangerous.

16. **connect** [to join; to place in a relationship]

This road **connects** the two towns.
Your head is **connected** to the rest of your body by your neck.

A: Is there a **connection** between those two companies?
B: No. They're not related.

17. **polite** [careful of other people and their feelings]

Her parents liked her boyfriend because he was very **polite**.
The **polite** taxi driver said, "Thank you," when we gave him the fare.
The rules of **politeness** differ from one country to another.

Introductory Exercises

A. Match each word with its definition.

____	1. to return to the earth	**a.**	angle
____	2. careful	**b.**	bend
____	3. the most important	**c.**	cautious
____	4. to separate into two or more groups	**d.**	connect
		e.	divide
____	5. the driver of an airplane	**f.**	fare
____	6. movement	**g.**	iron
____	7. to join; to place in a relationship	**h.**	jet
		i.	land
____	8. with no change in direction	**j.**	main
____	9. a metal made from iron	**k.**	motion
____	10. a change in direction	**l.**	pilot
____	11. careful of other people and their feelings	**m.**	polite
		n.	steel
____	12. a very fast airplane	**o.**	straight
____	13. the money you pay for a trip in a taxi, bus, train, etc.		

B. Answer each question with a word from the word form chart in this unit.

1. What kind of plane flies very fast?
2. What do you pay when you enter a bus?
3. How do parents teach their children to behave?
4. What metal is found in the ground?
5. What does a jet do at the end of a flight?
6. How should you cross the street?
7. What do students learn after they learn multiplication?
8. What do you see when something moves?
9. Who drives a jet?

Study Exercises

C.   Write **T** if the sentence is true and **F** if it is false.

_____ **1.** You can move something by pulling it.

_____ **2.** You will get hurt if you are too cautious.

_____ **3.** Two things which are connected have a relationship.

_____ **4.** A solid piece of iron will float on water.

_____ **5.** Nice people are polite.

_____ **6.** If you have one cake and eight guests, you need to divide the cake into at least eight or nine pieces.

_____ **7.** The main street in a town is an important street.

_____ **8.** Cars are made partly of steel.

_____ **9.** Jets are a slow way to travel.

_____ **10.** Some metals bend.

D.   Match each word with its opposite.

_____ **1.** bent

_____ **2.** cautious

_____ **3.** connected

_____ **4.** divide

_____ **5.** main

_____ **6.** polite

_____ **7.** pull

_____ **8.** straight

    a. unrelated
    b. join
    c. straight
    d. unimportant
    e. metal
    f. push
    g. pilot
    h. impolite
    i. careless
    j. bent

E.   Circle the word which is different in meaning.

1. multiply   add   bend   divide

2. jet   train   plane   pilot

3. fare   gold   iron   steel

4. fee   fare   price   connection

5. polite   nice   main   kind

6. connect   divide   join

7. motion   movement   iron

F. Read the passage and answer the questions that follow.

     The government Office of Transportation announced this morning that major construction would occur on the main road connecting the country's two largest cities. Two important improvements are to be made. First, an iron
5 divider is to be constructed in the middle of the four-lane road. Second, several of the worst bends in the road are to be reconstructed, making the road straighter. The government hopes that these two changes will make this main road much safer; however, the Office of Transportation also added that if
10 people drove more cautiously, these changes would not be necessary.

1. On which road will the construction occur? _____

_____

2. What will be built in the center of the road? _____

_____

3. What else about the road will be changed? _____

_____

4. What is the purpose of these changes? _____

_____

5. How else could safety on the road be improved? _____

_____

Follow-up

G. Dictation: Write the sentences that your teacher reads aloud.

1. _____

2. _____

3. _____

4. _____

5. _____

H. Answer the following questions.

  1. Are you a cautious driver? How do you drive cautiously?
  2. How much are the bus fares in your city?
  3. What are the main cities in your country?
  4. Is iron found in your country? Where?
  5. Does your country produce steel? Where are the factories?
  6. Are bus drivers and taxi drivers in your country polite? Why do you
     think so?
  7. Have you ever had motion sickness? When? How can people avoid
     motion sickness?
  8. Which cities in your country have airports where large jets can land?
  9. By what forms of transportation are the major cities in your country
     connected to each other?

I. Complete the stories.

  1. John is not a cautious driver . . .
  2. Mary is in New York. She needs to arrive in Los Angeles within
     eight hours . . .

UNIT
3

Work (A)

Word Form Chart

NOUN	VERB	ADJECTIVE	ADVERB
		actual	actually
appointment	appoint	appointed	
criteria			
department			
export	export	exported	
exportation			
	fire	fired	
		gradual	gradually
income			
ladder			
optimist		optimistic	optimistically
optimism			
output			
partner			
partnership			
personnel			
project			
promotion	promote	promoted	
retirement	retire	retiring	
		retired	

Definitions and Examples

1. **income** [the money received for work or from other sources during a period]

    Her yearly **income** from her job and from interest is more than $30,000.

    Americans must pay taxes on all their **income**.

2. **fire** (a) [to dismiss]

    The boss **fired** him because he always came to work late.

    He was **fired** last month and still has not found a new job.

    "**Fire**" is a less formal word than "dismiss."

    (b) [assumed: the heat and light produced when something burns]

    John started a **fire** to keep himself warm.

3. **promote** [to raise to a higher position or office]

    The company has **promoted** her twice in the last three years.

    Her most recent **promotion** was one month ago.

    If he is not **promoted** soon, he plans to get a job with another company.

4. **retire** [to stop working, usually because one is old]

    He **retired** when he was 60 years old.

    It is a good idea to save money to use after your **retirement**.

5. **appoint** [to choose someone to do a job]

    The boss **appointed** me to investigate the problem.

    He was **appointed** by the president to head the Office of Transportation.

6. **appointment** [a time agreed for a meeting]

    I have an **appointment** for a job interview at 10:00 A.M. tomorrow.

    He was late for the **appointment**, and the boss was angry.

7. **export** [to sell things to another country]

    The United States **exports** a lot of wheat to other countries.

    The Middle Eastern countries **export** oil.

8. **partner** [a person who does something with someone else]

    My business **partner** handles the export part of our company.

    He and his tennis **partner** have won many of their matches.

9. **department** [a separate part of a business or government]

   He works in the sales **department** of the company.
   She is the head of her **department**.

10. **personnel** [the people who work for a business]

   The **personnel** at that company receive high salaries.
   The **personnel** department of a company makes the decisions about whom to employ.

11. **project** [a plan to work on]

   The company is working on a **project** for the government.
   We work in the same department, but presently we are working on different **projects**.

12. **output** [how much a person or business produces]

   The **output** of that factory is very high because it is efficient.
   We need to increase our **output** to make a profit.

13. **optimistic** [with a positive attitude about the future]

   We are **optimistic** that the company will succeed.
   He is an **optimist**. He always thinks that the future will be good.

14. **gradual** [happening slowly]

   The growth of that company has been **gradual**. It grows a little bit larger each year.
   The company increases the workers' wages **gradually**, year after year.

15. **ladder** (a) [moveable steps]

   The painter used a **ladder** to reach the ceiling.

   (b) [positions in a company, arranged according to rank]

   Very good employees usually go up the **ladder** of success quickly.

16. **criteria** {singular: criterion} [the factors used to make a decision]

   A worker's output is one of the **criteria** used in making promotion decisions.
   The most important **criteria** used to decide a worker's salary in that company are his age and the efficiency of his work.
   In that country, there is only one **criterion** of success: how much money you make.

17. actually [really]

He looks poor, but **actually** his income is high.
That country **actually** exports most of the cars which it produces.

Introductory Exercises

A.   Match each word with its definition.

_____ **1.** to sell things to another country
_____ **2.** a person who does something with someone else
_____ **3.** to stop working because one is old
_____ **4.** to raise to a higher position or office
_____ **5.** the money received for work or from other sources during a period
_____ **6.** happening slowly
_____ **7.** a factor used to make a decision
_____ **8.** to dismiss
_____ **9.** the people who work for a business
_____ **10.** a separate part of a business or government
_____ **11.** with a positive attitude about the future
_____ **12.** a plan to work on
_____ **13.** how much a person or business produces
_____ **14.** really

a. actually
b. appointment
c. criterion
d. department
e. export
f. fire
g. gradual
h. income
i. ladder
j. optimistic
k. output
l. partner
m. personnel
n. project
o. promote
p. retire

B.   Answer each question with a word from the word form chart in this unit.

   1. What do countries sometimes do with extra food which they produce?
   2. What do people do at the end of their careers?

3. What is a salary?
4. What might an employer do to a bad worker?
5. What do people who build houses use?
6. If you cannot do something by yourself, what do you need?
7. What should you not be late for?
8. What do employers want a lot of from their workers?
9. Who always thinks that the future will be better?
10. What may an employer do to a good employee?

Study Exercises

C. Write **T** if the sentence is true and **F** if it is false.

_____ 1. Young people often retire.

_____ 2. Your wages are part of your income.

_____ 3. Someone who is appointed is chosen by an election.

_____ 4. Something which happens gradually occurs quickly.

_____ 5. Personnel and sales are two possible departments in a company.

_____ 6. People want to be fired.

_____ 7. Partners usually help each other.

_____ 8. Employers promote all of their employees.

_____ 9. Bad employees always climb the ladder of success in their companies quickly.

_____ 10. Optimists are afraid of the future.

D. Match the words which are similar in meaning.

_____ 1. actually

_____ 2. appoint

_____ 3. criteria

_____ 4. department

_____ 5. fire

_____ 6. gradually

_____ 7. personnel

a. factors
b. argue
c. really
d. dismiss
e. slowly
f. staff
g. negotiate
h. part
i. choose

E. Complete each sentence with a word from the word form chart in this unit.

    1. Japan _____ a lot of automobiles.

    2. My aunt works in the personnel _____ of that company.

    3. That factory is very efficient; its daily _____ is very high.

    4. She was _____ to the position of president two months ago.

    5. The output of that factory is _____ increasing; each year it produces a little more.

    6. The two _____ own equal shares of that company.

    7. That company is having trouble with its _____ ; the workers have been on strike for a week.

    8. She is 60 years old, so she is planning to _____ soon.

    9. People with high _____ are often rich.

   10. He used a(n) _____ to reach the second floor windows.

F. Read the passage and answer the questions that follow.

       Harry went to the personnel department of the Phoenix Corporation yesterday for a job interview. His appointment was at 10:00 A.M., and the interview finished at 10:45. He is not sure that he got the job, but he is optimistic about his
5 chances. The interviewer told him that the most important criteria for hiring were the applicants' college grades and previous work experience.

       After the interviewer asked Harry about his education and work experience, she gave him the opportunity to ask
10 her some questions about the company. Harry was pleased to learn that the Phoenix Corportation takes good care of its employees. There are many opportunities for a hard worker to gradually climb the corporate ladder, and each promotion brings an increase in income. In addition, the company has a
15 good retirement program to protect its older workers.

       Harry is especially excited about the idea of working for the Phoenix Corporation because of a major export project currently being started there. If he is hired, Harry hopes to be assigned to this project. Although Harry has applied at
20 several other companies, Phoenix is his first choice.

1. Where did Harry go for his interview at Phoenix? _____

   _____

2. Why did he have to be there at 10:00 A.M.? _____

   _____

3. What two criteria does the company use in its hiring? _____

   _____

4. What two advantages do workers at Phoenix have? _____

   _____

5. What work at Phoenix does Harry want to be assigned to? _____

   _____

Follow-up

G. Dictation: Write the sentences that your teacher reads aloud.

   1. _____

   2. _____

   3. _____

   4. _____

   5. _____

H. Answer the following questions.

   1. How important is it to be on time for appointments in your country? Is ten minutes late considered to be actually late?
   2. What are the most important criteria for promotion in companies in your country?
   3. What products does your country export? To where?
   4. For what reasons are workers fired in your country?
   5. What is the average income in your country in the cities? In the country?
   6. Are you generally optimistic in your life?
   7. Name some situations in which you have had a partner.

8. At what age do people usually retire in your country? Is retirement at this age required?
9. If you could choose, at what age would you retire? Why?

I.   Describe the work life and retirement situation of . . .

1. a typical factory worker in your country.
2. a typical company executive in your country.

Vacation

Word Form Chart

NOUN	VERB	ADJECTIVE	ADVERB	PREPOSITION
adjustment	adjust	adjusted		
		adjustable		
canvas				
cliff				
compromise	compromise			
echo	echo	echoing		
extent	extend	extended		
extension		extensive	extensively	
	flex	flexible	flexibly	
		flexed		
luxury	luxuriate in	luxurious	luxuriously	
native		native		
occupant	occupy	occupied		
		occupying		
pioneer	pioneer	pioneering		
		plain	plainly	
		primitive	primitively	
tension	tense	tense	tensely	
		tensed		
tent	tent			
tribe		tribal		
				toward(s)

Definitions and Examples

1. **primitive** [of the earliest times; simple; original]

   Our summer house is **primitive**; it does not have water or electricity.

   A: Do you like **primitive** camping?
   B: Yes. It's very relaxing to get away from modern life for a short time.

2. **tent** [a cloth house]

   Sleeping in a **tent** can be fun.

   A: Does this campground have a special area for **tents**?
   B: Yes. It's over there.

3. **canvas** [a heavy cloth used to make sails and tents]

   A **canvas** tent is strong but is sometimes heavy.

   A: Why did you buy **canvas** tennis shoes?
   B: **Canvas** shoes are lighter than leather ones.

4. **cliff** [a side of a hill that is high and almost straight up and down]

   Cliffs can be dangerous to climb.

   A: Let's camp by the **cliff**.
   B: It's safer by the river, unless it floods!

5. **echo** [a sound which is sent back or repeated from a surface]

   If you talk loudly near those cliffs, you can hear an **echo**.

   A: I feel nervous alone in the forest.
   B: Yes. Especially when you hear that strange **echo**.

6. **extend** [to make longer]

   If we are having fun, we can **extend** our trip.

   Student: Can I have an **extension** on my paper? I can't finish it by the due date.
   Teacher: All right. I'll **extend** the due date one week.

7. **flexible** [able to bend, move or change easily, without breaking]

   Small trees are **flexible**. Even in strong winds they do not break.

   A: Let's go to Florida next month.
   B: No. Next month is too soon!
   A: OK. I'm **flexible**. We can go whenever you want.

8. **compromise** [an agreement in which each side wins a little and loses a little]

   If you are flexible, you can often reach a **compromise**.

   A: I want Chinese food tonight.
   B: I want Italian food!
   A: We can **compromise**. Tonight, Chinese food, and tomorrow, Italian.

9. **luxury** [an expensive or rare thing that gives comfort or pleasure]

   I like **luxuries**. I want to have a big car and expensive clothes.

   A: This hotel is really **luxurious**.
   B: And expensive, too, I'll bet!

10. **occupy** [to live in; to fill up or to take up a place]

    Is this hotel room **occupied**, or is it empty?

    A: Which camping space do you like?
    B: I like the one by the lake, but it looks **occupied**.

11. **native** [someone who lived in a place originally, or was born there; something that was found in a place originally]

    Native Americans are called Indians.

    A: I'm lost. Where are we?
    B: I don't know. Let's ask a **native** to give us directions.

12. **pioneer** [someone who is the first to enter and live in a region; someone who leads the way in thought and study]

    When the **pioneers** went into space, no one knew what they would find.

    A: This forest is very primitive.
    B: Yeah! I feel like a **pioneer**.

13. **tribe** [a group of people united by language, social customs, and ancient family ties]

    Americans Indians have a **tribal** organization.

    A: I'd like to visit Arizona and New Mexico.
    B: Me, too. I hear there are some Native American **tribes** that still live there.

14. **tense** [not relaxed; causing or showing excitement or stress]

    If we cannot compromise, there will be a lot of **tension**.

    A: I came to Rio to relax.
    B: You were really **tense** before, but now you seem happy.

15. **adjust** (a) [to change in order to make right or better]

    A: That light is too bright!
    B: I'll **adjust** it so it doesn't hurt your eyes.

    (b) [to become used to]

    It was difficult to **adjust** to our new life in Tokyo.

16. **plain** [not fancy; simple; ordinary or average]

    Raj likes people who are **plain** and simple because they are easy to live with.

    A: Do you like to stay in luxury hotels on your vacations?
    B: No. I prefer **plain** hotels. A clean bed in a small room is enough for me.

17. **toward(s)** [in the direction of, to]

    If you drive west from Miami, you are going **toward** the Gulf of Mexico.

    A: Let's drive **toward** home tonight.
    B: Yes. We can find a hotel if it gets late.

Introductory Exercises

A. Match each word with its definition.

____	1. someone born in a place	**a.** adjust
____	2. a cloth house	**b.** canvas
____	3. in the direction of	**c.** cliff
____	4. to take up a place	**d.** compromise
____	5. not fancy	**e.** extend
____	6. the first person to enter new lands	**f.** flexible
____	7. not modern and new	**g.** luxury
____	8. a straight hill of rock or earth	**h.** native
____	9. a type of agreement	**i.** occupy
____	10. to make longer	**j.** pioneer
____	11. an expensive and comfortable thing	**k.** plain
		l. primitive
		m. tent
		n. toward

B. In the blanks, write the appropriate word(s) from the word form chart in this unit.

1. Tents are often made from _____ .

2. You can sometimes hear your voice _____ in the woods.

3. The mountain range _____ to the ocean.

4. Expensive clothes, furs, and fancy cars are _____ .

5. If someone is staying in a room, that room is _____ .

6. A(n) _____ American is called an Indian.

7. Groups of people who are not modern are often called

   _____ .

8. After driving for three hours in heavy traffic, you may feel

   _____ .

9. If you drive southwest from Toronto, Canada, you are driving

   _____ Niagara Falls.

10. This material will bend easily because it is _____ .

11. I like _____ food; I don't enjoy fancy restaurants.

12. When you move to a new place, it takes time to

   _____ .

13. If we don't agree, we try to _____ .

Study Exercises

C. Write **T** if the sentence is true and **F** if it is false.

_____ 1. Pioneers are natives of the place where they are pioneering.

_____ 2. Tribes no longer exist.

_____ 3. If you flex your arm, you hurt yourself.

_____ 4. You can adjust your television if the picture is bad.

_____ 5. You read or watch TV in order to feel tense.

_____ 6. If you like plain living, you like luxuries.

_____ 7. An extensive vacation is a long one.

_____ 8. If you fall off a cliff you could hurt yourself.

_____ 9. A compromise is a way to end a disagreement.

_____ 10. An echo is a repetition of a sound.

D.   **I.** Write the word from the word form chart in this unit which is the opposite of the word given.

  1. relax _____

  2. poverty _____

  3. modern _____

  4. fancy _____

  5. inflexible _____

II. Write the word from the word form chart in this unit which is the synonym of the word or phrase given.

  1. explorer _____

  2. bend _____

  3. make longer _____

  4. repeat _____

  5. fill _____

E.   In the blanks, write the appropriate word(s) from the word form chart in this unit.

A good vacation to take if you like to travel for (1) _____ periods of time is a camping trip. To enjoy such a trip, you should also enjoy (2) _____ living, food cooked outdoors, and lots of exercise. A necessity for your trip is a good (3) _____ . It should be light enough to carry, but made of a strong cloth like (4) _____ . At first, you will need time to (5) _____ to the new environment: camping is very different from staying in a (6) _____ hotel. If you are (7) _____ , you will adjust quickly, and you will find that camping is a good way to relax after (8) _____ city living.

Follow-up

F.   Dictation: Write the sentences that your teacher reads aloud.

1. _____

2. _____

3. _____

4. _____

5. _____

G.   Answer the following questions.

1. Has it taken you long to adjust to your English class? Why or why not?
2. Do you have anything made of canvas?
3. What are the natives of your country called?
4. What do you do when you feel tense?
5. Are there any tribes in your country?
6. Have you ever heard an echo? Where?
7. Do you like primitive camping? Why or why not?
8. Have you ever slept in a tent? When?
9. Do you prefer luxurious or plain living? Explain.
10. When you disagree with someone, do you usually try to compromise? Why or why not?
11. Are you a flexible person? Explain.
12. Are there any modern pioneers? Who are they, and where do they go?

H.   1. Tell what it would be like to be a pioneer.
2. Describe a vacation you have had recently.
3. Imagine you are going camping. Describe what you would do and where you would go.

Media

Word Form Chart

NOUN	VERB	ADJECTIVE	ADVERB
comparison	compare	comparative	comparatively
constancy		constant	constantly
editor	edit	edited	
		editing	
editorial			
evil		evil	evilly
fold	fold	folded	
		folding	
illustration	illustrate	illustrated	
illustrator			
implication	imply	implied	
		implicit	implicitly
index	index	indexed	
issue	issue	issuing	
		issued	
journal			
journalism			
journalist		journalistic	journalistically
list	list	listed	
quotation	quote	quoted	
report	report	reported	reportedly
reporter		reporting	
reputation		reputed	reputedly
significance	signify	significant	significantly
insignificance		insignificant	insignificantly
suggestion	suggest	suggested	

Definitions and Examples

1. **report** [a factual description or statement about one topic]

    My history teacher wants us to write a two-page **report** about the Civil War.

    Newspaper and TV **reporters** provide the public with news.

    A: Did you hear the weather **report** this morning?
    B: Yes. They said that it's going to rain all day.

2. **edit** (a) [to correct a piece of writing]

    When you **edit** a report, you can correct spelling, add words, and organize paragraphs differently.

    (b) [to correct and organize a book, magazine, or newspaper for publication]

    A newspaper **editor** makes the final decisions about which articles will be printed.

    An **editorial** states the opinion of the **editor**.

3. **journal** (a) [a magazine or newspaper]

    Doctors read medical **journals** for current information about health.
    Journalists are writers who report or edit the news.
    Young people who want to work for a newspaper study at a **journalism** school.

    (b) [a daily record of activities]

    During my vacation, I kept a **journal** of my thoughts and experiences.

4. **illustration** [a picture or example which makes something clear]

    This vocabulary book has **illustrations** for some words.
    The speaker gave several examples to **illustrate** his idea.

5. **suggest** [to put an idea in another person's mind]

    Editors **suggest** topics for articles to reporters.

    A: I need some information about personal computers.
    B: Why don't you look at some computer journals in the library?
    A: That's a good **suggestion**. I'll go tomorrow.

6. **imply** [to suggest an idea without saying it directly]

    By not printing the article, the editor **implied** that it was not important.

    A: Do you think the president will send the army to that country?
    B: That was the **implication** of his speech, but he didn't actually say it.

7. **issue** (a) [a topic of discussion or argument]

    The Vietnam War was an important **issue** in the United States for many years.

    (b) [one printing of a journal]

    The current **issue** of <u>Time</u> magazine contains a report on primitive tribes in Australia.

8. **compare** [to study or describe similarities and differences]

    Before you buy something expensive, you should **compare** the prices at several stores.
    This report is a **comparison** of Eastern and Western attitudes about families.
    Compared to most Asians, people in the United States speak loudly.

9. **constant** [continuous; not changing]

    The workers complained about the **constant** noise in the factory.
    Reporters must work **constantly** to get the most current news.

10. **evil** [very, very bad]

    Some religions teach that **evil** people go to hell.
    Murder is one of the most **evil** things people do.

11. **fold** [to bend in such a way that one part is on top of or next to another part]

    If you **fold** that paper, the computer cannot accept it.
    A newspaper may be **folded** in the middle or on the side.

12. **list** [many names, words, or numbers, written one after another]

    I usually write a shopping **list** before I go to the market.
    Everyone who has a telephone is **listed** in the phone book.

13. **index** [an alphabetical list of topics, showing the page for each one]

    A book's **index** is usually at the end, but in a newspaper the **index** may be on the first page.

    A: Does this book have any information about the steel industry?
    B: I don't know—look for "steel" in the **index**.

14. **quote** [to report someone's exact words]

> Newspapers frequently **quote** government officials.
> A **quotation** is printed between **quotation** marks. "I promise to improve the government" is a **quotation**.

15. **reputation** [the quality of a person or thing, according to people in general]

> This newspaper has an excellent **reputation**. Everyone thinks that the reporting is fair and complete.
> A: Have you ever been to that restaurant?
> B: No, but I suggest that you avoid it. It has a terrible **reputation**.

16. **significant** [important]

> Newspapers print the most **significant** stories on the first page. Today's editorial explains the **significance** of the government's decision.

Introductory Exercises

A. Match each word with its definition.

____ 1. a magazine or newspaper	**a.** compare
____ 2. a picture or example	**b.** constant
____ 3. to suggest indirectly	**c.** edit
____ 4. to bend	**d.** fold
____ 5. an alphabetical list	**e.** illustration
____ 6. a factual description	**f.** imply
____ 7. to describe similarities and differences	**g.** index
	h. issue
____ 8. continuous	**i.** journal
____ 9. important	**j.** quote
____ 10. a topic of discussion	**k.** report
____ 11. to report someone's exact words	**l.** reputation
	m. significant
____ 12. to put an idea in someone's mind	**n.** suggest

B. Answer each question with a word from the word form chart in this unit.

1. Where can you find the page for a subject in a book?
2. What is a picture to explain something?
3. What is a report of someone's exact words?
4. What do you often do to paper before you put it in an envelope?
5. What has many reports on one subject?
6. What gives the opinion of a journalist in a newspaper?
7. What is an indirectly stated idea?
8. What kind of people do very bad things?
9. What is the general name for a reporter or editor?
10. What is a description of similarities and differences?
11. What are people's ideas about the quality of someone or something?
12. What can you take with you when you go shopping, so that you don't forget to buy some things?

Study Exercises

C. Write **T** if the sentence is true and **F** if it is false.

_____ 1. There are three illustrations on this page.
_____ 2. Lazy people are constantly busy.
_____ 3. Paper is easy to fold.
_____ 4. This book has an index at the end.
_____ 5. Religions help people to be evil.
_____ 6. A quotation always ends with a question mark(?).
_____ 7. Most people want to have a good reputation.
_____ 8. Reporters usually write about insignificant issues.
_____ 9. The sun shines constantly.
_____ 10. Newspapers are folded one or more times.
_____ 11. Compared to the United States, England is a big country.

D. In the blanks, write the appropriate word(s) from the word form chart in this unit.

1. I want to be a reporter, so I'm going to study _____ .
2. I bought this car because the company has a good

_____ .

3. This professor's lectures are very clear. He gives several examples to _____ each idea.

4. Getting married is a _____ change in a person's life.

5. My friend asked for my advice, so I gave him several _____ .

6. Before you buy something expensive, you should _____ the prices at different stores.

7. The current _____ of <u>Newsweek</u> magazine has a report on African politics.

8. Today's editorial _____ that the president is wrong, but it doesn't disagree with him directly.

9. The entertainment pages of the newspaper included a(n) _____ of movies.

10. I can never find anything in that book. It doesn't have a(n) _____ .

E.   Circle the word which is different in meaning.

1. imply   suggest   compromise
2. evil   bad   fair
3. significant   adequate   important
4. issue   illustration   picture
5. sudden   constant   continuous
6. journalist   personnel   reporter
7. index   list   title
8. bend   break   fold

F.   Write the correct words in the blanks.

ACROSS

1. not important
6. a list of topics
8. journalists
9. with pictures
10. a newspaper employee
11. words or names in order
12. continuous

DOWN

2. gave someone an idea
3. similarities and differences
4. bend
5. the opinion of the newspaper's editor
6. an indirect suggestion
7. to give the exact words
8. quality, according to public opinion

Follow-up

G. Dictation: Write the sentences that your teacher reads aloud.

1. _____

2. _____

3. _____

4. _____

5. _____

H. Give a short answer to each question.

1. Name some things that fold easily.
2. Name two internationally-known people who have good reputations and two who have bad reputations.
3. Does your city's newspaper have an index? Where is it printed?
4. Do newspapers in your native language contain many quotations? From whom?
5. Compare two newspapers that you know. Talk about their appearance, their use of illustrations, their political ideas.
6. Name one current political issue in your country.
7. What is the most significant news story in your country this week?
8. What are some characteristics of a good journalist?
9. What suggestions can you give to a student who wants to learn vocabulary?

I. Your local newspaper has asked you to write an article. You may write about any issue that you consider significant. Describe what you will write about.

Health

Word Form Chart

NOUN	VERB	ADJECTIVE	ADVERB
belly			
cancer		cancerous	
chart	chart	charted	
consciousness		conscious	consciously
		unconscious	unconsciously
consultation	consult	consulting	
consultant			
		crazy	crazily
diagnosis	diagnose	diagnostic	diagnostically
drowning	drown	drowned	
energy	energize	energetic	energetically
epidemic			
faint	faint	fainting	
germ			
infection	infect	infectious	
		infected	
lungs			
mark	mark	marked	
pallor	pale	pale	
recovery	recover	recovered	
		recovering	
	sharpen	sharp	
		tiny	

Definitions and Examples

1. **pale** [not having much color]

     He was **pale** from his illness.
     You should get out in the sun more; you are very **pale**.

2. **belly** [stomach]

     If you eat meat which is bad, you will get a pain in your **belly**.
     He had a big **belly** from drinking beer.

3. **conscious** [alert; awake]

     The patient was **conscious**, but too sick to talk.
     The man was **unconscious** when they pulled him from the car after
       the accident.

4. **faint** [to lose consciousness for a short time]

     Sometimes people **faint** if it is very hot, if they are very hungry, or
       if they see blood.
     He **fainted** and hit his head on the chair when he fell.

5. **tiny** [very small]

     Some insects are **tiny**; you can hardly see them.
     The **tiny** baby had been born the day before.

6. **germ** [something very tiny that causes sicknesses]

     Doctors are always washing their hands to avoid **germs**.
     People catch diseases from other people because of **germs**.

7. **infection** [a sickness caused by germs that can be passed to another
   person]

     He has a bad **infection** in that cut on his leg; the cut is **infected**.
     If a disease is **infectious**, one person can get it from another person.

8. **lungs** [the two things in your chest which you breathe with]

     Smoking cigarettes is bad for your **lungs**.
     People breathe with their **lungs**.

9. **drown** [to die by breathing in water]

     The little girl fell into the swimming pool and **drowned**.
     The **drowned** man had water in his lungs.

10. **epidemic** [the situation in which a large number of people have the same disease at the same time]

   > An **epidemic** in the fourteenth century killed almost half the population of Europe.
   > My mother's uncle died in an **epidemic** in 1917.

11. **recover** [to get better when you are sick]

   > I still have a cold, but I am **recovering** now.

   > A: Will she **recover**?
   > B: The doctor isn't sure. She may die.

12. **cancer** [a very serious, non-infectious disease which can be in many parts of the body]

   > Many victims of **cancer** do not recover.
   > A lot of researchers are trying to find a cure for **cancer**.

13. **consult** [to get advice or help from someone or a book]

   > If you are sick, you should **consult** a doctor.
   > She **consulted** a dictionary to find the meaning of the word.

14. **crazy** (a) [mentally ill]

   > Sometimes **crazy** people have to stay in mental hospitals.

   (b) [foolish]

   > It is **crazy** to drive too fast.

15. **diagnosis** {plural: diagnoses} [the decision about what illness a person has]

   > A: What is the **diagnosis**?
   > B: I'm afraid it's cancer.

   > The doctor **diagnosed** his condition as a stomach problem.

16. **energy** [the strength or power to work]

   > People who are sick do not have much **energy**.
   > Food is the fuel which gives people **energy**.
   > The sun, oil, and gasoline are all sources of **energy**.

17. **sharp** (a) [having an end or edge which cuts easily]

   > Be careful! That knife is very **sharp**.

   (b) [sudden or quick]

   > He felt a **sharp** pain in his belly, but it quickly disappeared.

18. **mark** [a spot or line that can be seen]

> The white paint left a **mark** on her dress.
> You can see the **mark** on her skin where she had the operation.

19. **chart** [a paper with listed information or illustrations]

> The nurse wrote the patient's temperature on his **chart**.
> The doctor studied the woman's **chart** before he examined her.
> The science classroom had many **charts** on the walls.

Introductory Exercises

A. Match each word with its definition.

_____ 1. alert; awake

_____ 2. to die by breathing in water

_____ 3. to decide what illness a person has

_____ 4. a paper with listed or illustrated information

_____ 5. the stomach

_____ 6. very small

_____ 7. to get better when you are sick

_____ 8. a very serious disease

_____ 9. to lose consciousness

_____ 10. not having much color

_____ 11. something very tiny that causes sicknesses

_____ 12. to get advice or help from someone or a book

_____ 13. the strength or power to do work

_____ 14. a spot or line

_____ 15. foolish; mentally ill

a. belly
b. cancer
c. chart
d. conscious
e. consult
f. crazy
g. diagnose
h. drown
i. energy
j. epidemic
k. faint
l. germ
m. infect
n. lungs
o. mark
p. pale
q. recover
r. sharp
s. tiny

B. Answer each question with a word from the word form chart in this unit.

1. What do doctors do to diseases?
2. Where do nurses write information?
3. What might you do if you do not eat for a long time?
4. How do you look when you are sick?
5. How large are germs?
6. During what do many people sometimes die at the same time?
7. What do you call it when an illness goes away?
8. What disease is very serious?
9. How do people die in water?
10. What might happen if a cut on your skin gets dirty?
11. What do you breathe with?
12. What are good knives?

Study Exercises

C. Write **T** if the sentence is true and **F** if it is false.

____ 1. Your lungs are near your heart.
____ 2. The sun makes people's skin pale.
____ 3. Cancer is an infectious disease.
____ 4. A person can recover after he drowns.
____ 5. People read charts.
____ 6. Consultants help people.
____ 7. A sharp knife cuts easily.
____ 8. Sick people are usually energetic.
____ 9. People often get pale when they faint.
____ 10. People with infections are crazy.

D. In the blanks, write the appropriate word(s) from the word form chart in this unit.

1. The child fell into the water and _____ .
2. He was very sick, but finally he _____ .
3. The doctor did many tests before he made the _____ .
4. The doctors are very busy now because there is a(n) _____ in the city.

5. You should _____ another doctor if you do not trust your current one.

6. Germs are so _____ that we cannot see them.

7. When she _____ , she fell to the ground.

8. The nurse showed the patient's _____ to the doctor, who read it carefully.

9. Her behavior is so strange that some people think that she is

_____ .

10. Because he smoked so much, he began to have trouble

with his _____ .

E.   Read the passage and answer the questions that follow.

Some people are so afraid of being told that they have cancer that they avoid going to the doctor for a diagnosis. My Aunt Josie is such a person.

She had severe pains in her belly for three weeks. During
5 that time she also lost all her energy. Then, one day, she fainted. When her husband found her unconscious, he rushed her to the hospital. When the doctor examined Aunt Josie, he had a surprising but happy diagnosis for her; instead of the cancer that she has been so afraid of, Aunt Josie had a simple
10 stomach infection. He promised her that with the medicine he gave her, she would recover within one week, and she did.

After her recovery, the family made Aunt Josie promise that she would never again be crazy enough to delay consulting a doctor for so long.

1. What diagnosis was Aunt Josie afraid of? _____

_____

2. How did she know that she was sick? (Two reasons)

a) _____

b) _____

3. Why did Aunt Josie's husband take her to the hospital? _____

_____

4. What was actually wrong with her? _____

_____

5. How long did her recovery take? _____

_____

6. What behavior did her family think was crazy? _____

_____

Follow-up

F. Dictation: Write the sentences that your teacher reads aloud.

1. _____

2. _____

3. _____

4. _____

5. _____

G. Answer the following questions.

1. When do you consult a doctor?
2. What do people in your country do when a person acts crazy?
3. Have you ever fainted? Why?
4. What do you do to avoid germs?
5. Have there been any epidemics in your city? When?
6. Do you ever get pale? When?
7. At what time of the day are you most energetic? Why?
8. What do you think is the best way to recover from a cold?
9. If a person faints, what should you do for him while he is unconscious?
10. Is cancer a very common disease in your country? Do doctors tell the patient that he or she has cancer, or do they tell only the family?

H. Complete the story.

John is very pale, and he says that he feels faint . . .

Housing

Word Form Chart

NOUN	VERB	ADJECTIVE	ADVERB
adequacy		adequate	adequately
inadequacy		inadequate	inadequately
antique		antique	
bulb (lightbulb)			
cabinet			
carpenter			
carpentry			
diagram	diagram	diagrammed	
district			
disturbance	disturb	disturbed	
		disturbing	
drawing	draw (drew, drawn)		
furnace			
gray		gray	
hammer	hammer	hammering	
		hammered	
inheritance	inherit	inherited	
		inheriting	
maintenance	maintain	maintained	
nail	nail	nailed down	
rug			
screw	screw		
screwdriver			
shelter	shelter	sheltering	
		sheltered	

Definitions and Examples

1. **cabinet** [a place to store things in a kitchen, bathroom, etc.]

   After he dried the dishes, he put them in the **cabinet**.

   A: Where are the coffee cups?
   B: In the **cabinet** over the sink.

2. **draw** [to make a picture]

   The child **drew** a picture of her house.
   That artist **draws** his pictures in pencil before he paints them.

3. **diagram** [a drawing which shows the exact shape and measurements of a building, machine, etc.]

   Trying to find the problem, the engineers carefully studied the
   diagrams of the equipment.
   The **diagram** of the house showed that it had two bathrooms.

4. **district** [an area of a city or country]

   Most people in this city do not live in its business **district**.
   The farming **district** of that country produces enough food to export
   to other countries.

5. **furnace** [a machine for producing heat for a building]

   Their house has a **furnace** in the basement.
   It is cold in our office today because the **furnace** is broken.

6. **gray** [a color between black and white]

   They painted the factory **gray**.
   On a cloudy day, the sky is **gray**.

7. **rug** [a carpet]

   That house has **rugs** on the floor of each of the rooms except the
   kitchen and the bathroom.
   A room with a **rug** on the floor feels warmer in the winter.

8. **nail** [a piece of metal used to hold pieces of wood together]

   Thousands of **nails** were used to construct that house.
   The little boy stepped on a **nail** and hurt his foot.

9. **hammer** [the tool used to force nails into wood]

   He used a **hammer** to hit the nail.
   She carefully **hammered** each nail into the roof.

10. **carpenter** [a person whose job is building things with wood]

    The **carpenters** are working on the roof of that new house now.
    We will need to hire a **carpenter** to put another window in our kitchen.

11. **disturb** [to bother]

    The noise of the carpenters' hammering early in the morning **disturbed** my sleep.
    The construction of that new house is **disturbing** the neighborhood.

    A: I heard a **disturbance** this morning. What was it?
    B: There was an accident in front of the house.

12. **screw** [a piece of metal used to hold building materials together]

    You turn a **screw** to put it in a piece of wood.
    The carpenter **screwed** each **screw** into the wall carefully.
    That cabinet is held on the wall by **screws**.
    If a **screw** is loose, you should **screw** it in tighter.

13. **screwdriver** [the tool used to turn screws]

    The carpenter used a **screwdriver** to tighten the screws holding the door.
    I need a tiny **screwdriver** to fix my glasses.

14. **antique** [very old; usually more than 100 years old]

    My grandmother has a lot of **antique** furniture in her house.
    Antiques are often worth a lot of money.

15. **inherit** [to receive something from a relative, often after the relative dies]

    We **inherited** this house from my grandfather when he died.
    Her **inheritance** was more than one million dollars.

16. **bulb** [the round, glass part of an electric light]

    This light needs a new **bulb**; it is not working.
    Do not drop that **lightbulb**; it will break.

17. **maintenance** [the keeping of something in good condition]

    The manager is in charge of the **maintenance** of this apartment building.
    If you want to sell this house in five years, you should **maintain** it as well as you can.

18. **adequate** [sufficient]

The maintenance of that building is not **adequate**; it is in poor condition.

This house has **adequate** space for a large family; it is large.

19. **shelter** [something that covers; a place of protection]

Some travelers knocked on our door during the storm because they needed **shelter**.

Everyone needs adequate food and **shelter**.

Introductory Exercises

A. Match each word with its definition.

_____ 1. the round, glass part of an electric light

_____ 2. to provide a cover or protection

_____ 3. a person whose job is building things with wood

_____ 4. sufficient

_____ 5. to bother

_____ 6. a color between black and white

_____ 7. an area of a city or country

_____ 8. to make a picture

_____ 9. a place to store dishes, glasses, etc., in a kitchen

_____ 10. a machine for producing heat in a building

_____ 11. a drawing which shows the exact shape and measurements of something

_____ 12. a carpet

_____ 13. the tool used to force nails into wood

_____ 14. very old

a. adequate
b. antique
c. bulb
d. cabinet
e. carpenter
f. diagram
g. district
h. disturb
i. draw
j. furnace
k. gray
l. hammer
m. inherit
n. maintenance
o. nail
p. rug
q. screw
r. screwdriver
s. shelter

B. Answer each question with a word from the word form chart in this unit.

   1. What heats a house?
   2. Name four things that a carpenter uses.
   3. Name part of an electric light.
   4. What do you find on the floor?
   5. What do people need during a storm?
   6. Name a color.
   7. What do you put dishes in?
   8. What may bother you?
   9. What is something that is very old?
  10. What is similar to a drawing?

Study Exercises

C. Write **T** if the sentence is true and **F** if it is false.

____ 1. When you inherit something, you lose it.
____ 2. The noise of hammering may disturb people.
____ 3. It is a good idea to maintain your house well.
____ 4. All rooms have rugs.
____ 5. People need adequate food and shelter.
____ 6. You use a furnace during the winter.
____ 7. Many young people have gray hair.
____ 8. Nowadays carpenters build antiques.
____ 9. People who build things may use diagrams to help them.
____ 10. Cabinets are used for storage.

D. Circle the word which is different in meaning.

   1. screw   antique   nail
   2. gray   rug   carpet
   3. diagram   carpenter   drawing
   4. adequate   sufficient   maintain
   5. shelter   district   area
   6. inherit   help   receive
   7. hammer   furnace   screwdriver
   8. disturb   bother   draw

E.   In the blanks, write the appropriate word(s) from the word form chart in this unit.

1. They painted the outside of their house _____ .

2. Which _____ of the city do you live in?

3. She took the dishes from the _____ .

4. I cannot see to read in this room; there is not _____ light.

5. If the light will not work, try changing the _____ .

6. People should not take _____ from thunderstorms under trees.

7. The child's mother was angry because he _____ on the wall.

8. From which side of the family did she _____ her blond hair?

9. When he tried to hit the nail with the _____ , he hit his finger instead.

10. The _____ for their house costs them a lot of money each year; it always needs repairs.

F.   Read the passage and answer the questions that follow.

      After living in an apartment for the first seven years of their marriage, Mary and Tom Hunter inherited twenty thousand dollars and some antique furniture from Mary's grandmother, and they decided to use the money as a down
5 payment on a house. They searched for houses in various districts of the city and finally found one that they liked.
      Unfortunately, the house had not been maintained adequately, and parts of it were in poor condition. However, Mary and Tom decided that because the house was in a good
10 neighborhood, it was worth the investment. So, they carefully examined the house and drew diagrams of how they wanted the inside of the house to be. Because they wanted major changes in the number and size of the rooms in the house, they hired a group of carpenters to do the work. While the
15 carpenters were working on the first floor of the house, Tom and Mary lived on the second floor. The constant hammering of the carpenters was disturbing to Tom, who worked at home, but he and Mary were happy that they had finally bought a house.

1. How did Mary and Tom get the money for the down payment on

the house? _____

_____

2. Where did they look for a house? _____

_____

3. Why were there some problems with the house? _____

_____

4. Whom did Mary and Tom hire to work on the house? _____

_____

5. What disturbed Tom when he worked at home? _____

_____

Follow-up

G. Dictation: Write the sentences that your teacher reads aloud.

1. _____

2. _____

3. _____

4. _____

5. _____

H. Answer the following questions.

1. Have you ever used a hammer and nails? For what purpose?
2. What is an adequate amount of money to buy a house in your city? To rent an apartment?
3. Do houses in your city usually have furnaces? Where?
4. Is there an inheritance tax in your country? How much?
5. Which district in this city has the most expensive houses?
6. Do you like to draw? What do you like to draw?
7. Are there rugs in any rooms in your house? Which ones?
8. What do you find disturbing in the neighborhood where you live now?
9. What type of antiques do people here collect?
10. Where should a person take shelter during a thunderstorm?

I. Describe the work of a carpenter.

Weather and Geography

Word Form Chart

NOUN	VERB	ADJECTIVE	ADVERB
contrast	contrast	contrastive	contrastively
		constrasting	contrastingly
dawn	dawn		
earthquake			
extremity		extreme	extremely
likelihood		likely	
		unlikely	
mildness		mild	mildly
notice	notice	noticeable	noticeably
peninsula		peninsular	
planet		planetary	
radar			
range	range		
recommendation	recommend	recommended	
reminder	remind		
sheet			
	slip	slippery	
softness	soften	soft	softly
steadiness	steady	steady	steadily
		unsteady	unsteadily
suffering	suffer		

Definitions and Examples

1. **extreme** [the greatest or highest]

    The climate here is not **extreme**; temperatures rarely go over 85° F or under 25° F.
    They have been having **extremely** hot weather since July.

2. **contrast** [something very different from something else]

    There is a great **contrast** between summer and winter.
    If you compare the weather here with the weather in my country, there is not much **contrast**.

3. **dawn** [the first light of morning]

    The temperature at **dawn** today was 75° F.

    A: What's the coolest time of day?
    B: The hours before **dawn**.

4. **earthquake** [sudden movements of the surface of the earth]

    A severe **earthquake** damaged buildings throughout the city.
    We had a minor **earthquake** last night. You could hardly feel it.

5. **planet** [a heavenly body that goes around the sun]

    Earth is a **planet**.

    A: What's the weather like here?
    B: I'd say we have the best weather of any place on the **planet**.

6. **likely** [probable]

    It is not **likely** that we will have snow in Florida in April.
    The **likelihood** of an earthquake in San Francisco is fairly great.

    A: Are you going to the park today?
    B: Not **likely**. Not in this weather.

7. **notice** [to see; to realize by seeing, feeling, tasting, etc.]

    You will **notice** the contrast between this color and that one.

    A: It's getting hot outside.
    B: I hadn't **noticed**.

8. **peninsula** [a narrow piece of land that extends out into the water]

> They have a house out on the **peninsula**.
> On one side of the **peninsula**, there is a very good beach.
> Florida is a **peninsula**.

9. **radar** [equipment that locates distant objects by radio waves]

> Airports need very good **radar** equipment.
> Pilots use **radar** to locate and avoid other airplanes.

10. **range** [the amount of variation]

> The amount of rainfall here is generally in the **range** of ten to twenty inches a year.
> The temperature today **ranged** from a low of seven to a high of only ten.

11. **recommend** [to advise]

> The weather forecast is not very good. I **recommend** that you bring an umbrella today.
> Her doctor **recommended** that she move to a dry climate.

12. **mild** [not extreme; not harsh]

> The climate in our area is **mild**. We do not have very hot or very cold weather.
> Yesterday was a **mild** spring day.

13. **remind** [to cause someone to remember]

> The professor **reminded** us that the exam is next week.
> The weather today **reminds** me of the weather we have back home.

> A: The phone company sent you a **reminder**.
> B: To **remind** me of what?
> A: You didn't pay last month's bill.

14. **sheet** (a) [a thin layer or surface]

> A **sheet** of ice covered the driveway.
> A thin **sheet** of water on the road caused the car to slide into a tree.

> (b) [a thin covering on a bed]

> A: Did you sleep with a blanket last night?
> B: No, only with a **sheet**.

15. **slip** [to slide accidentally]

> My foot **slipped** on the ice.
> When the water froze, the road became very **slippery**.

16. soft (a) [not hard]

   She was not injured. She just fell into the **soft** snow.

   (b) [not loud]

   I could not hear what he said. He spoke too **softly**.

17. steady [constant; continuous]

   We had a **steady** rainfall all morning.
   It snowed **steadily** for three hours.

18. suffer [to feel pain; to experience something painful]

   My mother **suffered** from heart disease.
   In war almost everybody **suffers**.

Introductory Exercises

A. Match each word with its definition.

____ **1.** early morning	**a.** dawn
____ **2.** a heavenly body that goes around a star	**b.** earthquake
____ **3.** the amount of variation	**c.** extreme
____ **4.** sudden movements of the surface of the earth	**d.** likely
____ **5.** to cause someone to remember something	**e.** mild
____ **6.** to feel pain	**f.** notice
____ **7.** constant; continuous	**g.** peninsula
____ **8.** probable	**h.** planet
____ **9.** to slide accidentally	**i.** radar
____ **10.** equipment that locates distant objects by radio waves	**j.** range
____ **11.** the greatest or highest	**k.** steady
____ **12.** to see	**l.** remind
	m. sheet
	n. slip
	o. suffer

B.   In the blanks, write the appropriate word(s) from the word form chart in this unit.

1. You should stay in school. That's my _____ .

2. We have to be concerned with international problems. We all live on the same _____ .

3. Living on a narrow _____ , she could walk to the beach.

4. The sky is clear blue. Rain is very _____ .

5. We'll get started early. Let's leave tomorrow at _____ .

6. The distant airplane could be seen on _____ .

7. To me 100° F is _____ hot.

8. He forgot his umbrella. I should have _____ him to take it.

9. After several hours of snowfall, the streets are very

   _____ .

10. All the buildings on this street were damaged in the

   _____ .

Study Exercises

C.   Write **T** if the sentence is true and **F** if it is false.

_____ 1. Many large airplanes carry radar equipment.

_____ 2. Our planet is called Earth.

_____ 3. A mild earthquake may not damage many buildings.

_____ 4. Streets are likely to be slippery on sunny days.

_____ 5. The frozen ground is soft in winter.

_____ 6. Tropical countries suffer from a lack of rainfall.

_____ 7. The geography of our planet is quite varied.

_____ 8. The weather forecaster recommends an umbrella on windy days.

_____ 9. Only countries in the northern hemisphere suffer frequent earthquakes.

D. Make sentences with the words.

1. extremely / rain / unlikely / is

   _____

2. us / radar / to forecast / helps / the weather

   _____

3. a sheet / the ground / covered / of ice

   _____

4. is / today / yesterday / noticeably / colder than

   _____

5. in the weather / didn't notice / I / the change

   _____

6. snowed / it / for two hours / steadily

   _____

7. an earthquake / suffered / at dawn / the peninsula

   _____

8. of temperature / extreme / is / the range

   _____

E. Circle the word which is different in meaning.

1. dawn   Earth   planet
2. notice   see   remind
3. morning   peninsula   dawn
4. mild   likely   probable
5. steady   soft   constant
6. suffer   advise   recommend
7. sheet   layer   range
8. peninsula   sun   land
9. slow   slip   slide

F.   Read the passage and answer the questions that follow.

       Weather and geography make San Francisco a pleasant but sometimes frightening place to live. Located on the end of a peninsula in northern California, the city enjoys a mild climate, although it is often cool and wet. San Francisco is

5 well-known for its fog, low temperatures, and rain, even in the summer. Residents may recommend that you bring sweaters and jackets even if you visit in July. Winter temperatures are not severe, however, for the weather is softened by the relatively warm air and water of the Pacific

10 Ocean.

       The weather of nearby areas is, in contrast, much warmer and drier. A few miles away from the ocean, the summers are very dry and free of fog. Daytime temperatures are sometimes 100° F. Winters are not very cold, and the

15 temperature rarely falls below freezing, even in January.

       While the climate is pleasant, the danger of earthquakes is not. As in many parts of California, earthquakes are a major worry of the people who live in the San Francisco area. In 1906, a powerful earthquake destroyed most of the city.

20 Residents know it is likely that an earthquake will happen there again. They know this, but they are not noticeably afraid of it. They seem to be accustomed to living with the danger. Some even take steps to prepare themselves by storing large amounts of food and other necessities and

25 constructing houses and buildings that can bear the stress that an earthquake may produce.

       Although there is danger, residents rarely leave in order to go to a safer area. "This is a beautiful place, and there are problems everywhere. No place is 100 percent safe," stated

30 one man who has spent his life in San Francisco.

1. Describe the weather in San Francisco. _____

_____

2. What do residents of the city recommend that you wear when you

come to visit? _____

_____

3. Why are the winters mild? _____

_____

4. How is the weather different outside the city? _____

_____

5. What are the people of California worried about? _____

_____

6. What happened in 1906? _____

_____

7. How do some people prepare for earthquakes? _____

_____

8. Why, in the opinion of one San Franciscan, is there no good reason

to leave the area? _____

_____

Follow-up

G. Dictation: Write the sentences that your teacher reads aloud.

1. _____

2. _____

3. _____

4. _____

5. _____

H. Listen to the definitions. Say the word from the word form chart in this unit that matches the definition.

1. the early morning
2. to cause someone to remember
3. to slide
4. not hard
5. probable
6. to show the difference between things
7. not severe
8. to see
9. equipment to detect objects at a distance
10. to experience pain
11. land extending into the ocean
12. a heavenly body that goes around a star

I. Answer the following questions.

1. How is the weather in your hometown?
2. Compare the weather here with that of your hometown.
3. What is your favorite season? Why?
4. Does your hometown suffer from extreme weather? If so, what kind?
5. What is the most dangerous kind of weather in this country?
6. How would you recommend that people dress in the winter here? In the summer?
7. Does the geography here remind you of home? In what way?
8. How does the geography here contrast with that of your home?

J. Tell a story about the following situation. What will happen?

It's a sunny June day. John is going to spend the weekend in San Francisco. He packs a small bag with swimwear and one change of clothes. He rushes to the airport.

Environment

Word Form Chart

NOUN	VERB	ADJECTIVE	ADVERB	PREPOSITION
shame	shame	ashamed		
		shameful	shamefully	
		shameless	shamelessly	
awfulness		awful	awfully	
				beneath
conservation	conserve	conserved		
		conserving		
definiteness		definite	definitely	
indefiniteness		indefinite	indefinitely	
demonstration	demonstrate	demonstrated		
		demonstrating		
disgust	disgust	disgusted	disgustedly	
		disgusting	disgustingly	
elimination	eliminate	eliminated		
		fit		
		unfit		
harm	harm	harmful	harmfully	
		harmless	harmlessly	
introduction	introduce	introductory		
mine	mine	mined		
		mining		
		proper	properly	
		solar		
technique				

Definitions and Examples

1. **awful** [terrible; extreme]

>The air pollution there is **awful**; it hurts to breathe.
>Some people got **awfully** sick from drinking that water; they almost died.

2. **conserve** [to save; to protect]

>The purpose of that park is to **conserve** the animal life living there.
>The government asked us to **conserve** water because this summer has been very dry.
>**Conservation** is important to protect our environment.

3. **harm** [to damage; to hurt]

>Pollution **harms** our environment.
>Many factories are **harmful** to the environment around them.
>That snake is **harmless**; it does not bite.

4. **solar** [related to the sun]

>That house is heated by **solar** power.
>That calculator is **solar** powered; you need light to use it.

5. **fit** (for) [appropriate]

>That water is **fit for** drinking; it is not polluted.
>This area is **unfit for** humans to live in; it is extremely hot and windy.

6. **beneath** [under]

>The ball rolled **beneath** the table.
>Some areas of the earth have precious metals **beneath** the surface.

7. **demonstrate** (a) [to show]

>The company **demonstrated** its new solar power system before a large audience.
>The amount of sickness in this district **demonstrates** that the water pollution levels are too high.

(b) [to publicly speak or act against something]

>A large group of people were **demonstrating** in front of the factory which had polluted the river.

8. **mine** [a deep hole in the ground from which diamonds, salt, silver, etc. are taken]

   There are many gold **mines** in South Africa.
   My uncle works in a **mine**, far beneath the surface of the earth.

9. **definitely** [for sure; certainly]

   The pollution in this area is **definitely** a problem; no one can argue that it is not serious.

10. **indefinitely** [for a period of time which is not certain but is often a long period]

    The mine will be closed **indefinitely** because of the accident; it may never open again.

11. **introduce** (a) [to make people known to each other]

    I was **introduced** to Mr. Brown at a business meeting.

    (b) [to bring into use]

    That mining company **introduced** the use of new equipment in its mine.

12. **technique** [a method; a way to do something]

    We need better **techniques** to remove pollutants from our water supply.
    That company introduced a new **technique** to use solar power.

13. **ashamed** [feeling guilty or bad about something]

    People should feel **ashamed** about polluting their environment.
    The little boy was so **ashamed** that he started to cry.

14. **disgust** [strong dislike]

    The townspeople are **disgusted** with the factory owners because of the pollution that the factory has caused.
    The people looked at the child's killer with **disgust**.

15. **eliminate** [to stop; to remove]

    We should try to **eliminate** the sources of pollution.
    The **elimination** of the pollutants in the river will make the water fit to drink.

16. **proper** [correct; appropriate]

    The factories should use **proper** methods to eliminate pollution.
    I do not know his name because we were not **properly** introduced.

Introductory Exercises

A.   Match each word with its definition.

      ____ **1.** to damage; to hurt

      ____ **2.** for sure; certainly

      ____ **3.** correct; appropriate

      ____ **4.** strong dislike

      ____ **5.** terrible; extreme

      ____ **6.** to save; to protect

      ____ **7.** to show; to publicly speak
or act against something

      ____ **8.** related to the sun

      ____ **9.** under

      ____ **10.** a deep hole in the ground
from which diamonds, salt,
silver, etc. are taken

      ____ **11.** a method

      ____ **12.** feeling guilty or bad
about something

a. ashamed
b. awful
c. beneath
d. conserve
e. definitely
f. demonstrate
g. disgust
h. eliminate
i. fit
j. harm
k. introduce
l. mine
m. proper
n. solar
o. technique

B.   Answer each question with a word from the word form chart in this unit.

1. Where can you find gold?
2. What kind of power comes from the sun?
3. What may pollution do to people and animals?
4. What may you feel when you see pollution?
5. How should someone feel who causes pollution?
6. What should we do to our environment?
7. What do people sometimes do when they dislike an action of the
government or a company?
8. What should we try to do to pollution?
9. What should you do when you meet someone for the first time?

Study Exercises

C. Write **T** if the sentence is true and **F** if it is false.

_____ **1.** People are happy about awful pollution.

_____ **2.** Water which is fit to drink will harm you.

_____ **3.** Many mines are beneath the ground.

_____ **4.** People do not like to feel shame.

_____ **5.** Something awful may disgust people.

_____ **6.** People demonstrate against things that they like.

_____ **7.** We should conserve good things.

_____ **8.** We should eliminate good things.

_____ **9.** Two weeks is an indefinite period of time.

_____ **10.** We need more techniques to eliminate pollution.

D. Match each word with its opposite.

_____ **1.** ashamed

_____ **2.** awful

_____ **3.** beneath

_____ **4.** conserve

_____ **5.** disgust

_____ **6.** fit

_____ **7.** harmless

_____ **8.** definite

a. on top of
b. love
c. inappropriate
d. uncertain
e. technique
f. nice
g. eliminate
h. dangerous
i. solar
j. proud

E. In the blanks, write the appropriate word(s) from the word form chart in this unit.

1. The mine was located hundreds of feet _____ the surface of the earth.

2. The use of solar power was _____ during this century.

3. The government asked the company to describe the _____ they were using to conserve power.

4. The executives of that company should be _____ of the amount of pollution they have caused.

5. The pollution in that river is _____ bad; the water is not fit to use.

6. The _____ against the company was reported on the news; the report said that hundreds of people stood outside of the factory.

7. We need to discover new techniques to _____ pollution.

8. That polluted water smells _____ .

F. Read the passage and answer the questions that follow.

A two-hour demonstration occurred yesterday outside the offices of the Bright Diamond Company. The demonstration, attended by about 500 angry people, was the public's answer to the company's recent announcement of its
5 new technique for mining diamonds. The company stated plans to introduce this new method, which will result in the destruction of large areas of wilderness land, in a forested region of the northwest United States.
American conservationists strongly oppose the plans of
10 the Bright Diamond Company, feeling that this new method of mining will leave the area unfit for wildlife for an indefinite period following the closing of the mine. The company, however, has stated that with proper care, the mined area could be returned to its wilderness condition
15 within twenty years after the end of the mining operation. A spokesman for the conservationists argued against this idea. He said that it was disgusting that the company wanted to continue with a plan which would bring immediate harm to the wildlife in the region and eliminate large areas of forest,
20 even if the damage could be repaired in the future.

1. What happened yesterday at the Bright Diamond Company?

Why? _____

_____

2. Who is against the company's plan? Why? _____

_____

3. What is the company's opinion about how long the damage will

last? _____

_____

4. What would the mining operation immediately eliminate? _____

_____

5. What would be harmed by the mine? _____

_____

Follow-up

G. Dictation: Write the sentences that your teacher reads aloud.

1. _____

2. _____

3. _____

4. _____

5. _____

H. Answer the following questions.

1. Does your country have mines? What kind? Where?
2. What kinds of pollution problems do the mines cause?
3. Have you ever demonstrated against anything? What?
4. What do you find to be disgusting? Why?
5. Have any types of pollution been eliminated in your country recently? How?
6. Is the water in the rivers and lakes in your country fit to drink? Why or why not?
7. Which type of pollution do you think is the most harmful in your country? Why?
8. Does your country have definite plans to eliminate pollution? What kinds of plans?
9. Is it polite in your country to introduce yourself to a stranger or is it more polite to wait for a third person to introduce you?
10. Is solar power used in your country? In what ways?
11. What would you like to eliminate from the world?

I. Describe any major efforts at conservation in your country. What things need to be conserved? Why? What techniques are used to conserve these things?

Clothing

Word Form Chart

NOUN	VERB	ADJECTIVE	ADVERB
attraction	attract	attractive	attractively
		attracted	
awareness		aware	
button	button	buttoned	
dye	dye	dyed	
		dying	
exchange	exchange	exchangeable	
femininity		feminine	femininely
		fine	finely
garment			
needle			
pattern	pattern	patterned	
pin	pin		
polish	polish	polished	
		polishing	
sewing	sew (sewed, sewn)		
	shrink (shrank, shrunk)	shrunken	
stretch	stretch	stretched	
		stretchy	
style	style	stylish	stylishly
thread	thread		
tradition		traditional	traditionally
	wear out (wore out, worn out)	worn out	

Definitions and Examples

1. **sew** [to work with material to make or repair clothes, curtains, etc.]

    A **sewing** machine is useful for making clothes.
    Poor quality clothes are not **sewn** well.

2. **needle** (a) [a small thin tool for sewing]

    You need a strong **needle** to sew leather.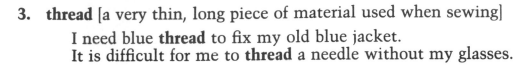

    (b) [the tool used by a doctor for putting medicine
       beneath a patient's skin]

    A doctor's **needle** must be clean and sharp.

3. **thread** [a very thin, long piece of material used when sewing]

    I need blue **thread** to fix my old blue jacket.
    It is difficult for me to **thread** a needle without my glasses.

4. **pin** [a thin, sharp thing used to hold articles together]

    It is easier to sew if you **pin** the pieces of material
       together first.

5. **attract** [to pull to oneself]

    The lions were **attracted** by the smell of meat.

6. **attractive** [pleasing]

    She looks very **attractive** in her new dress.

7. **attraction** [a thing that interests people; a force that holds things
    together]

    The fast food shop was the biggest **attraction** in the neighborhood.

8. **aware** [knowing]

    New babies are sometimes not **aware** of other people.
    We were not **aware** of the rain until we went outdoors.

9. **button** (a) [a small, often round, flat thing used to
    close clothing]

    My coat is missing a **button**.

    (b) [a thing that is turned or pushed to make something work]

    If you push the **button**, the engine will start.

10. **dye** [something used to give color to cloth, hair, food, etc.]

My sister **dyed** her hair black.
Vegetable **dye** is used in some foods.

11. **exchange** [to change; to give something for something else]

If the jacket does not fit, you can **exchange** it for the right size.
I usually **exchange** gifts with my husband on our anniversary.

12. **feminine** [having to do with women and girls]

"Actress" is the **feminine** form of "actor".
Some people think that housework is a **feminine** activity.

13. **fine** (a) [very good; excellent; high quality]

He has **fine** clothing from expensive shops.

(b) [very small or thin]

I need my glasses when I read **fine** print.

14. **garment** [a piece of clothing]

I took six **garments** to the dry cleaner.
This **garment** is intended for outdoor wear.

15. **pattern** (a) [a model for something to be made]

Dress **patterns** are sold in many shapes and sizes.
He tried to **pattern** his life after the life of a famous general.

(b) [the way in which things are arranged]

My wallpaper has an interesting flowered **pattern**.

16. **polish** [to make smooth and shiny]

He **polishes** his new car every weekend.
I need to buy shoe **polish** because my shoes are dirty.

17. **shrink** [to make or become smaller]

Wool **shrinks** in hot water.
Class enrollment is **shrinking** every year; each year we have fewer
    students.

18. **stretch** [to make or become longer or wider; to extend or cause to
extend]

She **stretched** out her arms to the small child.
Can you **stretch** these shoes to fit me?

19. **style** [a personal or special type of pattern or way of expressing and performing]

    That author has a very clear and direct writing **style**.
    What shoe **style** do you like best?

20. **stylish** [a way of dressing or behaving that is considered fashionable]

    Stylish clothing can be very expensive.

21. **tradition** [ideas, customs, and beliefs that have been passed down from age to age]

    The **traditional** costumes from that village are very colorful.
    In the United States, the **traditional** Thanksgiving meal includes
        sweet potatoes.

22. **wear out** (a) {separable} [to use until no longer useful]

    Cotton **wears out** more quickly than leather.
    These shoes are too old. I **wore** them **out** last year.

    (b) [tired from an activity]

    I am **worn out** from so much exercise.

Introductory Exercises

A. Match each word with its definition.

____ **1.** high quality	**a.** attractive
____ **2.** a tool for sewing	**b.** aware
____ **3.** a piece of clothing	**c.** dye
____ **4.** to make smaller	**d.** fine
____ **5.** knowing	**e.** garment
____ **6.** pleasing; charming	**f.** needle
____ **7.** a model	**g.** pattern
____ **8.** fashionable	**h.** polish
____ **9.** used to give color	**i.** proper
	j. shrink
	k. stylish
	l. tradition

B. Answer each question with a word from the word form chart in this unit.

1. What do you use to close your jacket?
2. What can you do if you buy the wrong size shirt?

3. What can we do to shoes that are not shiny?
4. What do we do with a needle and thread?
5. What kind of meals are often eaten on holidays?
6. What can you do if your new shoes do not fit?
7. What does a doctor use to give shots?
8. What would you like to do to boots that are too small?
9. What can you use to change the color of your hair?
10. What are dresses, coats, shirts, skirts, etc.?

Study Exercises

C. Write **T** if the sentence is true and **F** if it is false.

_____ 1. Bees are attracted by flowers.

_____ 2. Garments are sold in a restaurant.

_____ 3. A sewing machine is used for cooking.

_____ 4. Both pins and needles are very fine.

_____ 5. We learn about traditions from our parents and grandparents.

_____ 6. Cold glass stretches easily.

_____ 7. You should keep your coat buttoned in the winter.

_____ 8. When you sleep you are usually not aware of the time.

_____ 9. You need thread to cut your hair.

D. In the blanks, write the appropriate word(s) from the word chart in this unit.

1. Some people think a high singing voice is very _____ .

2. I was not _____ of the earthquake. I was sleeping.

3. If you push the _____ , the bell will ring.

4. I _____ the furniture when I clean the house.

5. The knees of my pants are _____ .

6. I hurt my finger with a _____ , and it's bleeding now.

7. I _____ my career after a famous businessman.

8. Business is decreasing. Each year the profits are

_____ .

E.   Circle the word or phrase which is different in meaning.

1. garment   atmosphere   clothing
2. deposit   pin   needle
3. polish   shine   exchange
4. traditional   thin   fine
5. charming   worn out   attractive
6. traditional   customary   shrunken
7. model   powder   pattern
8. knowing   aware   dyed

F.   Read the passage and answer the questions that follow.

My cousin Charlotte is a very attractive young woman.
She is always aware of the latest fashions and enjoys buying
fine clothes. Charlotte is always properly dressed, and her
shoes are always polished. Sometimes she chooses
5   traditional, feminine clothing for work, but for parties she
chooses more stylish clothing. Charlotte takes good care of
her clothes, too. They never look stretched, shrunken, or
worn out.
Recently, however, Charlotte decided that she was
10   spending too much money on her clothes. Now she is taking
sewing lessons and hopes to make some simple garments for
herself. She has selected a skirt pattern and has pinned the
pattern pieces to the material. She chose wooden buttons,
but later exchanged them for leather buttons. The last time I
15   saw Charlotte, she was threading her needle. The next time
maybe I will see her wearing her new skirt.

Write **T** if the sentence is true and **F** if it is false.

＿＿ 1. Charlotte is not interested in clothes.
＿＿ 2. Charlotte's shoes are sometimes dirty.
＿＿ 3. Charlotte chooses stylish clothes for parties.
＿＿ 4. Charlotte is careless about her clothes.
＿＿ 5. Charlotte spends a lot of money on clothes.
＿＿ 6. Charlotte is taking music lessons.
＿＿ 7. Charlotte is sewing a dress.
＿＿ 8. Charlotte chose buttons made of metal.
＿＿ 9. Charlotte's garment is finished.

Follow-up

G. Dictation: Write the sentences that your teacher reads aloud.

1. _____

2. _____

3. _____

4. _____

5. _____

H. Answer the following questions.

1. What kinds of things can you use polish on?
2. Do brides wear traditional garments in your country? Describe them.
3. What kinds of activities are considered feminine?
4. Have you patterned your life after a famous person? Who?
5. Are the latest hair styles attractive? Why or why not?
6. What color would you like to dye your hair?
7. What should you do if you buy the wrong size?
8. Do you wear out your shoes quickly? How?
9. What are the proper garments for cold weather?
10. How can you avoid shrinking your sweaters?
11. Do you know how to sew a button back on your shirt? What do you use to do it?
12. Are you aware of fashion changes?

I. 1. Describe the process of making a garment.
2. Describe traditional feminine clothing in your country.

Farming

Word Form Chart

NOUN	VERB	ADJECTIVE	ADVERB
circumstance		circumstantial	circumstantially
crisis			
decade			
enormity		enormous	enormously
		even	evenly
fertilizer	fertilize	fertilized	
		fertilizing	
herd	herd	herded	
pasture			
pipe	pipe	piped	
plenty		plentiful	plentifully
possession	possess		
possessor			
prosperity	prosper	prosperous	prosperously
		prospering	
resource		resourceful	resourcefully
settler	settle	settled	
settlement			
soil			
string			
	tie	tied	
wire	wire	wired	

Definitions and Examples

1. **decade** [a period of ten years]

   There have been improvements in farming techniques during each of the last six **decades**.

   The **decade** of the 1950s was a good one for American farmers.

2. **enormous** [very large]

   That farm is **enormous**; it covers many square miles of land.

   That farmer made an **enormous** profit by selling his crops at an excellent price.

3. **herd** [a group of animals, for example, sheep, cows, or horses]

   That **herd** of cattle contains more than 300 cows.

   Some of the sheep in that **herd** are sick.

4. **pasture** [a field with grass for animals]

   Our herd of cattle is in the north **pasture** today because the grass is good there.

   A: Which **pasture** is larger?
   B: Oh, the east **pasture** is enormous.

5. **fertilizer** [a substance used to increase the growth of crops]

   Most modern farmers spend a lot of money buying **fertilizers** to use on their crops.

   The **fertilizer** which I used helped these plants grow very rapidly.

6. **possess** [to own]

   That farmer **possesses** several large pastures.

   When he died, he left his **possessions** to his children.

7. **soil** [dirt which can be used to grow plants]

   The **soil** in this region is excellent for growing many types of crops.

   The **soil** in that area is so rich that it is not necessary to use much fertilizer.

8. **crisis** {plural: crises} [a major problem]

   The year 1986 was a time of **crisis** for American farmers: many lost their farms.

   The lack of rain will soon cause a **crisis** here; the crops will begin to die.

9. **pipe** [a long, thin piece of metal or other substance, with a hole for carrying a liquid or a gas]

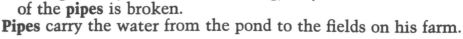

> The irrigation system is not working; maybe one
>   of the **pipes** is broken.
> **Pipes** carry the water from the pond to the fields on his farm.

10. **plenty** [a lot of; enough]

> That farmer has **plenty** of pastures for his herds; the animals have
>   more than enough to eat.
> The farmers are happy when rain is **plentiful**.

11. **prosper** [to do well; to make a profit]

> At first their farm had some trouble, but for the past five years it
>   has **prospered**.
> That **prosperous** farmer possesses enormous herds of cattle and
>   sheep.

12. **circumstance** [a situation]

> Lack of rain is a difficult **circumstance** for farmers.
>
> A: Under what **circumstances** would you sell your farm?
> B: I wouldn't sell it under any **circumstances**!

13. **string** [a long, very thin piece of material]

> The areas of the different vegetables in my garden
>   are separated by pieces of **string**.
> She used some **string** to hold the box closed.

14. **wire** [a string-like material made of metal]

> There is a **wire** fence around the pasture.
> There were no telephone **wires** leading into the house; they had no
>   phone.

15. **even** [without differences in level; smooth]

> The surface of the large pasture was very **even**; there were no rocks
>   or high areas.
> The farm's profit is not **even** from year to year; some years it is
>   high, and other years it is low.

16. **resource** [the useful things that a person, area, or country has]

> The natural **resources** which farmland should have are rich soil and
>   plenty of warm weather and rain.
> The old man had no **resources** left; his family had died and his
>   money was gone.
> She is very **resourceful**. She can always find a way around any
>   problem.

17. **settle** [to go to a place and stay there]

   The travelers **settled** in an area with excellent natural resources: good soil and plenty of rain.
   A: Where will you **settle**?
   B: Anywhere that I can find work.

18. **tie** [to put together with string, thread, or similar material]

   He **tied** his horse to a tree in front of our house so that it would not run away.
   The robber **tied** the victim's hands behind his back.

Introductory Exercises

A. Match each word with its definition.

_____ 1. without differences in level

_____ 2. very large

_____ 3. a period of ten years

_____ 4. to go to a place and stay there

_____ 5. a group of animals

_____ 6. a substance used to increase the growth of crops

_____ 7. to do well; to make a profit

_____ 8. a lot of; enough

_____ 9. a field with grass for animals

_____ 10. a major problem

_____ 11. dirt which can be used to grow plants

_____ 12. a situation

_____ 13. a string-like material made of metal

a. circumstance
b. crisis
c. decade
d. enormous
e. even
f. fertilizer
g. herd
h. pasture
i. pipe
j. plenty
k. possess
l. prosper
m. resource
n. settle
o. soil
p. string
q. tie
r. wire

B. Answer each question with a word from the word form chart in this unit.

   1. What can water travel through?
   2. What is the opposite of "tiny"?
   3. How should the surface of a road be?

4. What helps a country to prosper?
5. What do you do if you find a place where you would like to live?
6. Where do farmers keep animals which eat grass?
7. What is a group of cows?
8. What can help crops grow?
9. What is ten years?
10. What is a serious problem?
11. What is the opposite of "not enough"?
12. What is something that you own?

Study Exercises

C. Write **T** if the sentence is true and **F** if it is false.

_____ 1. People enjoy crises.

_____ 2. People want to prosper.

_____ 3. An even road is difficult to drive on.

_____ 4. An enormous group of flowers is a herd.

_____ 5. An area with many resources should prosper.

_____ 6. Farmers never use fertilizer in any circumstances.

_____ 7. Farmers use string around their pastures to keep the animals in.

_____ 8. Prosperous people usually have plenty of possessions.

_____ 9. Wires can carry electricity.

_____ 10. A two-year-old child can always tie his shoes.

_____ 11. Wires and pipes can carry water.

D. In the blanks, write the appropriate word(s) from the word form chart in this unit.

1. Some countries are poor because they lack natural _____ .

2. The death of his _____ of cattle from disease was a real _____ for the farmer.

3. That farmer should use plenty of _____ because the soil on his farm is not rich enough.

4. The old _____ in that farmhouse make a lot of noise when you turn on the water.

5. European people first _____ in the eastern part of the United States.

6. There has been no rain, and the temperature has been over 100° F. Under these _____ many of the crops will die.

7. The child _____ a string around the cat's neck, but the animal easily broke it.

8. The farmers are discussing the _____ caused by low crop prices with government advisors.

9. The farmer won a prize for growing the largest vegetables; some of his vegetables were really _____ .

E.   Read the passage and answer the questions that follow.

The summer of 1986 was a time of crisis for many farmers in the United States. A variety of circumstances combined to create major problems for them.

During the early part of the decade, crop prices had
5   begun to decrease. Farmers had been producing enormous quantities of crops, and inside the United States, their products had become too plentiful, causing the prices to fall. At the same time, prices for fertilizers rose. This combination of factors had decreased the prosperity of many
10   farmers by 1986.

However, the real crisis for the farmers in that year was caused by the weather. Farms in the southeastern part of the country received no rain during the spring and the first two months of the summer. Even, yearly rainfalls are usually one
15   of the resources of the southeast, and, therefore, most of the farms did not have adequate irrigation systems. As the grass in their pastures became dry and brown in late July, the southeastern farmers realized that they might lose most of their herds and go out of business.
20   Many farmers did in fact go out of business and were forced to sell all of their possessions, including their herds and land, to pay their bills. However, some farms in the southeast were saved when farmers in other areas of the country, who were having a prosperous year, sent them free
25   hay for their herds. The combination of August rain and help from more prosperous farmers saved many southeastern farms from the crisis of 1986.

1. Why did crop prices decrease during the early 1980s? _____

_____

2. What happened to the price of fertilizer during the early 1980s? _____

_____

3. Why did the farmers in the southeast not have irrigation

systems? _____

_____

4. Without rain, what happened to the pastures? _____

_____

5. What happened to the farmers who went out of business? _____

_____

6. Why were some farmers in other areas able to send free hay to the

crisis area? _____

_____

Follow-up

F. Dictation: Write the sentences that your teacher reads aloud.

1. _____

2. _____

3. _____

4. _____

5. _____

G. Answer the following questions.

1. Has this decade been a prosperous one for farmers in your country? Explain.
2. Which areas of your country are the most heavily settled? Why?
3. Name some things that wire is used for.
4. What is your family's proudest possession? Why?
5. Describe the worst crisis that your country has faced.

6. How old were you when you learned to tie your shoes by yourself?
7. Under what circumstances did you decide to study English?
8. Is the rainfall in your city even throughout the year or heavier during some months? Explain.
9. Do most farmers in your country use fertilizers?

H. Describe the resources which your country has and those which it lacks.

Government

Word Form Chart

NOUN	VERB	ADJECTIVE	ADVERB
agency			
agent			
aid	aid		
authority	authorize	authorized	
balance	balance	balanced	
		balancing	
benefit	benefit	beneficial	
border	border	bordering	
contradiction	contradict	contradictory	
		contradicting	
		contradicted	
emigration	emigrate	emigrating	
emigrant			
establishment	establish	established	
document	document	documented	
immigration	immigrate	immigrating	
immigrant			
insistence	insist	insistent	insistently
policy			
progress	progress	progressive	progressively
		progressing	
protest	protest	protesting	protestingly
protester		protested	
restriction	restrict	restrictive	restrictively
		restricted	
		restricting	
society	socialize	social	socially
socialization			

NOUN	VERB	ADJECTIVE	ADVERB
stability	stabilize	stabilized	
		stable	
instability		unstable	
trade	trade	trading	
		traded	

Definitions and Examples

1. **border** [the edge of a geographical area]

   The United States shares **borders** with Mexico and Canada.

   It is difficult for citizens of some countries to cross the **border** into neighboring countries.

2. **aid** [help]

   Many governments give **aid** to their poorer citizens.

   The victims of the fire were **aided** by their friends and neighbors.

3. **document** (a) [an official paper]

   We had to show our **documents** in order to cross the border.

   Many important historical **documents** are stored in that museum.

   (b) [to show or prove]

   The police asked me to **document** my location at the time of the murder.

   His writings **document** the history of the town.

4. **immigrate** [to come into a country to stay permanently]

   Many Europeans **immigrated** to the United States in the early 1900's.

   Most governments control the number of **immigrants** to their countries each year.

   You need documents from the United States embassy to **immigrate** to the United States.

5. **emigrate** [to leave a country to live permanently somewhere else]

   My grandparents **emigrated** from France to the United States.

   Many **emigrants** from Ireland and Scotland went to the United States to find a better life.

6. progress [advancement]

> There has been much **progress** in the peace talks; the war may end soon.
>
> The government should help the country to **progress** and become a better home for its citizens.

7. restriction [a limitation]

> The United States government has **restrictions** on how many immigrants may enter the country each year.
>
> Many governments **restrict** their citizens' carrying of weapons; some governments do not allow any weapons, but others allow small weapons.

8. policy [a general plan which has been decided on]

> The government's **policy** on crime may change when the new president takes office.
>
> A: What is your country's **policy** on immigration?
> B: It's very strict; there are many restrictions.

9. protest [to speak or act publicly against something]

> A large crowd of people **protested** outside the government building, angry at the new policy on food prices.
>
> Some governments permit peaceful **protest**; others do not.
>
> When the **protesters** became violent, they were arrested by the police.

10. trade (a) [the buying and selling of agricultural or manufactured products between countries]

> The United States has **trade** agreements with many nations.
> During the early 1980s, many countries attempted to increase **trade** with China.

(b) [to give one object to get another object]

> The little boy **traded** some toys with his friend.
> I **traded** my old car for a new one.

11. stable [not changing]

> A **stable** government will help that country progress.
> The value of that country's money is **unstable**; this week it is worth only half of what it was worth last week.

12. **authority** (a) [official power]

> The president has more **authority** than anyone else in the country.

(b) [a person with official power]

> The immigration **authorities** did not permit her to enter the country.

13. **agency** [an administrative division of the government]

> The Defense **Agency** of that country manages the country's military.
> That **agency** has authority over all foreign trade.

14. **agent** [a person who makes arrangements for his employer]

> Our **agent** has arranged for a meeting with the two other companies.
> That company has **agents** in cities all over the world.
> He was arrested for being a secret **agent** for another government.

15. **society** [a community or nation having common traditions and interests]

> Immigrants sometimes have trouble getting accustomed to the new **society** in which they are living.
> She became a doctor because she wanted to help **society**.

16. **establish** [to bring into existence]

> The government wants to **establish** a new immigration policy.
> Many countries **established** trade with China during the 1970s.

17. **insist** [to demand; to say strongly]

> The protesters **insisted** on speaking with the president.
> The government **insists** that it is making progress on the trade problems.

18. **balance** [to keep steady or even]

> Countries want to have a **balance** of trade with their trading partners; if one country exports much more than the other, there is no **balance**.
> The government must **balance** the positive and negative factors before deciding on a policy.

19. benefit (a) [to do good for]

The new government policy will **benefit** the poor people by
lowering food prices.
A stable government **benefits** the whole country.

(b) [an advantage]

Some countries offer immigrants many **benefits**, such as job
training and language lessons.

20. contradict [to go against a person in what he says]

The speech by the leader of the protest **contradicted** what the
president had said.
That document does not make sense; there are too many
contradictions in it.

Introductory Exercises

A. Match each word with its definition.

_____ **1.** an official paper

_____ **2.** to speak or act publicly
against something

_____ **3.** advancement

_____ **4.** the edge of a geographical
area

_____ **5.** a general plan which has been
decided on

_____ **6.** to come into a country to
stay permanently

_____ **7.** not changing

_____ **8.** to leave a country to live
permanently somewhere else

_____ **9.** to bring into existence

_____ **10.** an administrative division
of a government

_____ **11.** to demand; to speak strongly

_____ **12.** official power

_____ **13.** to go against a person
in what he says

_____ **14.** to keep steady or even

_____ **15.** an advantage

a. agency
b. aid
c. authority
d. balance
e. benefit
f. border
g. contradict
h. document
i. emigrate
j. establish
k. immigrate
l. insist
m. policy
n. progress
o. protest
p. restrict
q. society
r. stable
s. trade

B. Answer each question with a word from the word form chart in this unit.

1. What can people do if they do not like a government decision?
2. What do you cross when you go from one country into another?
3. What do countries do with their extra grain?
4. What do you call a foreigner who comes to live in your country permanently?
5. What does the government try to do to crime?
6. What is an important paper?
7. What is something that is good for you?
8. What does a person do if he wants you to believe something?
9. What should you give to someone who needs help?
10. What do you do if you disagree with someone and you state your opinion?
11. If you leave your country to live permanently in another country, what are you?

Study Exercises

C. Match each word with the word most similar in meaning.

_____	1. aid	**a.**	edge
_____	2. authority	**b.**	plan
_____	3. benefit	**c.**	help
_____	4. border	**d.**	paper
_____	5. establish	**e.**	advantage
_____	6. document	**f.**	limit
_____	7. policy	**g.**	start
_____	8. progress	**h.**	unchanging
_____	9. restrict	**i.**	advance
_____	10. stable	**j.**	power

D. In the blanks, write the most appropriate word(s) from the word form chart in this unit.

1. A person who works for his government and steals secrets from another government is a secret _____ .
2. The constitution of a nation is a very important _____ .

3. In addition to a good salary, the government workers receive
   excellent _____ , such as health insurance and paid
   vacation time.

4. The president was angry because the _____ made so
   much noise that the rest of the audience could not hear his speech.

5. The government has restricted _____ with that country
   because of disagreement with its import tax policies.

6. The United Nations gives millions of dollars of _____
   to the poorer countries each year.

7. The United Nations was _____ during World War II.

8. The president of a nation has much more _____ than an
   ordinary policeman.

9. The government must _____ the spending it does with
   the taxes which it collects.

10. A country with a _____ government can probably make
    more progress than one whose leaders change every few months.

11. Countries which do not have good control over their borders
    have difficulty in restricting _____ .

12. The president is _____ that his new policy be followed
    exactly.

E.   Read the passage and answer the questions that follow.

        The Immigration and Naturalization Service (INS) is the
     United States government agency which has authority over
     foreign people who want to settle permanently in the United
     States. Although policies on immigration are established by
5   the elected representatives in the national government, the
     job of the INS is to make sure that these laws are followed.
     The duties of an INS agent might be guarding a United States
     border or processing immigration documents.
        The purpose of the United States immigration policy is
10   to benefit all of the United States society by balancing the
     number of immigrants from each country. However, many
     citizens and people who want to immigrate feel that some of
     the restrictions on immigration are not fair. Protesters
     against the current immigration policy insist that restrictions
15   on the numbers of immigrants from each country should be
     based on the number of people wanting to emigrate from the
     country.
        The attitudes of American citizens toward immigration
     differ. Some Americans remember that their grandparents
20   were immigrants and recognize that the talents and skills of
     many immigrants have helped the country progress. These

Americans may also want to aid those people's search for a
new life. Other Americans protest that the benefits of
immigration are not sufficient compared to the problems
25 which sometimes result. Perhaps the most common
complaint about immigration is that some citizens think that
they have lost their jobs to recent immigrants. However,
although Americans may disagree on immigration, the
United States will probably continue to be a "nation of
30 immigrants."

1. Whom does INS have authority over? _____
   _____

2. Give two examples of jobs of immigration agents. _____
   _____
   _____

3. What is the purpose of United States immigration policy? _____
   _____

4. Give two reasons why many Americans favor immigration. _____
   _____
   _____

Follow-up

F. Dictation: Write the sentences that your teacher reads aloud.

1. _____

2. _____

3. _____

4. _____

5. _____

G. Answer the following questions.

1. Who is the highest authority in your country?
2. What kinds of benefits do government workers receive in your country?
3. What countries border on your country?
4. What kind of official documents must people in your country carry with them?
5. How much immigration does your country permit? How much emigration? What are the restrictions?
6. What recent government policy are most people in your country happy about? Angry about?
7. Which countries does your country have the most trade with? Why?
8. In what areas is it most important that your country make progress rapidly?
9. Name some government agencies in your country. In which area does each have authority?
10. Did your country have a positive or negative balance of trade last year? Why?
11. Do many people emigrate from your country? Where do they go?

H. Discuss any border restrictions that your country has. Are documents necessary to cross the border? Is free trade over the border permitted? What are the benefits of these policies?

Science

Word Form Chart

NOUN	VERB	ADJECTIVE	ADVERB	PREPOSITION
atom		atomic	atomically	
botany		botanical	botanically	
botanist				
cement	cement			
classification	classify	classified		
		classifiable		
class	class			
circumference				
concrete				
cone		conical		
core				
crack	crack	cracked		
cube				
dimension		dimensional		
illumination	illuminate	illuminating		
		illuminated		
isolation	isolate	isolating		
		isolated		
mankind				
minus				minus
plus				plus
rectangle		rectangular		
rotation	rotate	rotating		
shape	shape	shaped		
triangle		triangular		

Definitions and Examples

1. **botany** [the scientific study of plants]

   Botany is one of the biological sciences.
   He knows the scientific names of many trees and other plants
   because he studied **botany**.

2. **classify** [to put into categories]

   A good botanist can **classify** any plant he examines.
   When you **classify** something into categories, the categories are
   called **classes**.

   A: What is the **classification** of that plant?
   B: I'm not sure exactly what kind it is.

3. **shape** (a) [the outer form of something]

   Most coins have a round, flat **shape**.
   The room was **shaped** like an "L."

   (b) [condition]

   My television is in bad **shape**. I need a new one.
   People can stay in **shape** by exercising daily.

4. **rectangle** [a shape with four sides and four equal angles]

   She drew a **rectangle** on the paper.
   My room is **rectangular** in shape.

5. **triangle** [a shape with three sides]

   Triangles which have one 90 degree angle are called
   are called right **triangles**.
   Most postage stamps are rectangular, but
   a few are **triangular**.

6. **dimension** [the measure of the length, width, or height of something]

   A line has only one **dimension**, length.
   A piece of furniture has three **dimensions**.
   A triangle is a two-**dimensional** shape.

7. **cube** [a three-dimensional shape with six flat, square
   sides of equal size, which meet at right angles]

   My room is exactly **cube**-shaped; it is ten feet long,
   ten feet wide and the ceiling is ten feet high.
   He put two **cubes** of sugar in his tea.

8. **cone** [a three-dimensional shape, similar to a triangle, with a circular base]

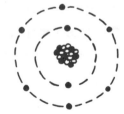

   The child loved to eat ice cream **cones**.
   He drank the water from a **cone**-shaped paper cup.

9. **core** [the central or most important part of something]

   He ate all of the apple except for its **core**.
   Scientists are not sure what is at the **core** of the Earth.
   The **core** courses in school are the important ones that all students take.

10. **cement** [a substance made from various powders and water, which dries to be hard like stone]

    Cement is used as a building material and to make sidewalks.
    She **cemented** the bricks together carefully.

11. **concrete** (a) [a building material made of cement, small stones, sand, and water]

    The apartment house was made of **concrete**.

    (b) [easily seen or understood]

    I understood her lecture because she used **concrete** examples.

12. **crack** [a small break or opening]

    There were **cracks** in the concrete wall.
    He dropped the dish, and it **cracked**.

13. **atom** [the smallest possible piece of a substance]

    Atoms are so tiny that they cannot be seen.
    Atom bombs are very powerful.

14. **circumference** [the outside edge of a circle; the distance around the edge of something]

    The **circumference** of the field was about 500 feet.
    The **circumference** of a circle is always at least twice as large as its diameter.

15. **illuminate** [to provide with light or knowledge]

    The single light bulb **illuminated** the whole room.
    That professor's lecture was very **illuminating**; I learned a lot.

16. **isolate** [to keep someone or something separate from others]

    Doctors sometimes **isolate** patients with infectious diseases.

    The farmhouse was quite **isolated**. The nearest neighbor was two miles away.

    Many students need **isolation** in order to study efficiently.

17. **mankind** [all human beings]

    A third world war might destroy **mankind**.

    Medical research attempts to help **mankind**.

18. **rotate** [to turn or cause to turn around a center]

    The wheels on a car **rotate**.

    The Earth **rotates** completely once each 24 hours.

19. **plus** (a) [added to; " + "]

    Five **plus** two equals seven.

  (b) [a little more than]

    Her grade was a "C **plus**."

20. **minus** (a) [made less by; " − "]

    Five **minus** two equals three.

  (b) [a little less than]

    His grade was a "C **minus**."

  (c) [negative]

    The temperature fell to **minus** twenty degrees Fahrenheit last night.

Introductory Exercises

A. Match each word with its definition.

_____ 1. the outer form of something

_____ 2. the central or most important part of something

_____ 3. the measure of the length, width, or height of something

_____ 4. the scientific study of plants

_____ 5. a small break or opening

_____ 6. to provide with light or knowledge

_____ 7. made less by

_____ 8. all human beings

_____ 9. to turn or to cause to turn around a center

_____ 10. added to

_____ 11. the outside edge of a circle

_____ 12. to put into categories

_____ 13. the smallest possible piece of a substance

a. atom
b. botany
c. cement
d. classify
e. circumference
f. concrete
g. cone
h. core
i. crack
j. cube
k. dimension
l. illuminate
m. isolate
n. mankind
o. minus
p. plus
q. rectangle
r. rotate
s. shape
t. triangle

B. Answer with a word from the word form chart in this unit.

1. What can you eat ice cream on?
2. Who studies plants?
3. Name two things that can be used to construct buildings.
4. What is every person on Earth a member of?
5. What is in the middle of an apple?
6. What two-dimensional shape has four sides?
7. What may happen to a cup if you drop it?
8. What does a light do to the area around it?
9. What two-dimensional shape has three sides?

Study Exercises

C. Write **T** if the sentence is true and **F** if it is false.

_____ **1.** A triangle has more angles than a rectangle.

_____ **2.** It is sometimes necessary to isolate a sick person.

_____ **3.** You can see atoms.

_____ **4.** A botanist classifies animals.

_____ **5.** You can measure a dimension.

_____ **6.** Concrete is made from cement.

_____ **7.** The diameter of a circle is smaller than its circumference.

_____ **8.** A fire can give illumination.

_____ **9.** The Earth rotates around the sun.

_____ **10.** "Plus" is the opposite of "minus."

_____ **11.** A triangle and a rectangle are both shapes.

_____ **12.** People want cracks in their windows.

D. Match each word with the one most similar in meaning.

_____ **1.** botany   **a.** light
_____ **2.** classify   **b.** turn
_____ **3.** class   **c.** biology
                                d. form
_____ **4.** crack   **e.** categorize
_____ **5.** illumination   **f.** humans
_____ **6.** isolate   **g.** separate
                                h. positive
_____ **7.** mankind   **i.** type
_____ **8.** minus   **j.** cement
_____ **9.** plus   **k.** negative
                                l. dimension
_____ **10.** rotate   **m.** break
_____ **11.** shape

E. In the blanks, write the appropriate word(s) from the word form chart in this unit.

1. He put two ice _____ in his glass of water.

2. The books in many libraries are _____ according to their topics.

3. Be careful not to break your mirror. Some people think that a _____ mirror means bad luck.

4. When new medicines are invented, most of _____ benefits.

5. _____ 50° F is a very cold temperature.

6. The carpenter used _____ to hold the bricks together.

7. I hate feeling _____ . I need to talk to other people frequently.

8. We need more _____ in this room; it is so dark I can't read.

9. The distance around the equator is the _____ of the earth.

10. The first _____ bombs were invented during World War II.

11. A cone is a three- _____ shape.

12. The change from night to day is caused by the _____ of the earth.

Follow-up

F. Dictation: Write the sentences that your teacher reads aloud.

1. _____

2. _____

3. _____

4. _____

5. _____

G. Answer the following questions.

1. Name some things that concrete is used for.
2. Have you ever felt isolated? When?
3. Name some things that rotate.
4. Have you ever experienced a temperature below zero? How low was it?
5. Name some things which are rectangular.
6. Would you like to study botany? Why or why not?

7. Does the grading system in your school use pluses and minuses?
8. What recent invention or discovery do you think has benefited mankind the most?
9. What were the core courses in your high school?

H.   Explain how shapes and forms can be classified. Use the following words: angles, dimensions, sides, surfaces.

Buying and Selling

Word Form Chart

NOUN	VERB	ADJECTIVE	ADVERB
grocer		grocery	
groceries			
label	label	labeling	
		labeled	
merchant			
merchandise			
			nearly
	obtain	obtained	
stock	stock	stocked	
		out of stock	
		in stock	
		particular	particularly
		quick	quickly
		relative	relatively
scheme	scheme	schematic	schematically
			seldom
series		serial	serially
specification	specify	specific	specifically
		specified	
standard	standardize	standard	
		standardized	
sum	sum	summed	
tendency	tend		
		ultimate	ultimately
		willing	willingly

Definitions and Examples

1. **groceries** [food and supplies]

   Jack's father was a **grocer**, and Jack worked in the family **grocery** store.
   I can carry only two bags of **groceries**.

2. **label** [a small piece of paper or cloth attached to something and giving information about the thing]

   The coat has a **label** inside to show the size and the manufacturer.
   A bottle of poison should be clearly **labeled**.

3. **merchant** [a person who buys and sells; a shopkeeper]

   I work as a clerk for a grain **merchant**.
   The **merchants** in my town advertise in the newspaper.
   A store should have new, good quality **merchandise**.

4. **nearly** [almost]

   It is **nearly** midnight. We should go home.
   He **nearly** fell off the ladder. He should be more careful.

5. **obtain** [to get]

   How can I **obtain** a driver's license?
   I hope to **obtain** a satisfactory grade in physics.

6. **stock** [a supply of merchandise or other items]

   The grocer does not keep a large **stock** of fresh fruit; it does not stay fresh very long.

7. **out of stock** [no longer available in the store]

   Out-of-stock merchandise can often be ordered.

8. **in stock** [available in the store].

   There are plenty of dictionaries **in stock** in the bookstore.

9. **particular** (a) [different from the others; special]

   I am busy at this **particular** time.
   We **particularly** like our journalism class.

   (b) [hard to please; very careful]

   He is very **particular** about his car. I do not think we should borrow it.

10. **specify** [to describe in detail; to say or name exactly]

> Did you **specify** any particular date for the meeting?
> He gave no **specific** reason for being late.

11. **relative** (a) [related or compared to each other]

> What are the **relative** advantages of cotton and wool?

> (b) [depending for meaning on a relation to something else]

> This is a **relatively** warm day for October.

12. **scheme** (a) [a plan or program for action, usually to do something negative]

> They **schemed** for months to rob the bank.

> (b) [in science, a plan for doing something]

> She showed me her **scheme** to easily remove gold from other metals.

13. **quick** [fast; happening in a short time]

> Please wait. I cannot walk so **quickly**.
> She took my hand and gave me a **quick** smile.

14. **series** [a number of similar things or events coming one after another]

> We heard a **series** of lectures by a famous professor.
> That author wrote a **series** of mystery stories.

15. **standard** (a) [a thing used as an example, a model, or an authority]

> His family has high **standards** of accomplishment.

> (b) [widely used; usual]

> Is this the **standard** fee for insurance?

16. **sum** (a) [the total; the complete amount]

> If you add these numbers, you will find the **sum**.

> (b) [an amount of money]

> My landlord asked for the **sum** of $300.

17. **tendency** [a thing that naturally happens; a preference to act in a certain way]

> Children have a **tendency** to cry when they are scared.
> Do you **tend** to be shy with strangers?

18. **seldom** [rarely; not often]

   It **seldom** snows in tropical places.
   I **seldom** write letters. I prefer to telephone my family.

19. **willing** [ready to and wanting to]

   We are **willing** to do any kind of work.
   Are you **willing** to let me borrow your bicycle?

20. **ultimate** [last; final; coming at the end; most basic]

   His **ultimate** ambition is to become a doctor.
   Ultimately, I would like to lose about twenty pounds.

Introductory Exercises

A.   Match each word with its definition.

_____ **1.** fast	**a.** groceries
_____ **2.** shopkeeper	**b.** label
_____ **3.** a program for action	**c.** merchant
_____ **4.** not available	**d.** nearly
_____ **5.** to get	**e.** obtain
_____ **6.** not often	**f.** out of stock
_____ **7.** food and supplies	**g.** particular
_____ **8.** a supply of items	**h.** quick
_____ **9.** very careful	**i.** scheme
_____ **10.** almost	**j.** seldom
_____ **11.** exact	**k.** series
	l. specific
	m. stock

B.   Answer each question with a word from the word form chart in this unit.

1. Who is the person who buys and sells?
2. What do you buy in a grocery store?
3. What do you get if you add numbers together?
4. What do you look at to see the size of a coat?
5. How might you describe someone who is hard to please?
6. What is another word for "rarely"?
7. What is a thing used as an example?
8. What do we call merchandise that is no longer available for sale?

Study Exercises

C. Write **T** if the sentence is true and **F** if it is false.

_____ **1.** Calculators can add very quickly.

_____ **2.** The wheel is a relatively recent invention.

_____ **3.** A good doctor is willing to help every patient.

_____ **4.** It seldom rains in the desert.

_____ **5.** The sum of twelve and eight is four.

_____ **6.** The meter is a standard measurement.

_____ **7.** Athletes have a tendency to be lazy.

_____ **8.** You can obtain good medical care in most large cities.

_____ **9.** Labels on food are good to eat.

_____ **10.** Professional pianists are very particular about their hands.

D. In the blanks, write the appropriate word(s) from the word form chart in this unit.

1. This is the third in a _____ of concerts by a famous orchestra.

2. I wanted to buy some oranges, but they were _____ . I bought apples instead.

3. My landlady has an interesting _____ for getting late rent.

4. If you want to be a successful farmer you have to be _____ to work long hours.

5. I _____ to feel sleepy on warm summer days.

6. Did the nurse _____ the time of your next appointment?

7. I like to shop in stores that sell a wide variety of _____ .

8. His bank says that he owes the _____ of $1,000.

9. _____ , it is the responsibility of parents to protect their children.

10. Last year I was so unhappy that I _____ quit my job.

E. Circle the word which is different in meaning.

1. sum   total   approval
2. final   humid   ultimate
3. foolishly   seldom   rarely
4. specific   severe   exact
5. residence   model   standard
6. expert   grocer   shopkeeper
7. nearly   almost   formally
8. get   classify   obtain
9. fast   quick   cruel
10. secret   particular   special

F. Read the passage and answer the questions that follow.

My grandfather told me that when he was a boy his ultimate aim was to be a merchant—specifically, a neighborhood grocer. As a young man, he had a scheme for obtaining a store, and he succeeded relatively quickly. That
5 is because my grandfather was willing to work long hours, and his store sold a wide range of merchandise. He was very particular about small things, like having correct labels. Also, he tended to spend large sums of money on improvements in his store.
10 My grandfather's dream was nearly ruined one year when a series of floods caused many foods to be out of stock for weeks—particularly the fresh fruits and vegetables. However, the business was ultimately a success, and I seldom go to a grocery store now without thinking of my grandfather.

1. What was my grandfather's ultimate aim? _____

_____

2. Did my grandfather succeed quickly? _____

_____

3. Why did he succeed? _____

_____

4. What was he particular about? _____

_____

5. What did he tend to spend a lot of money on? _____

_____

6. How was his dream nearly ruined? _____

_____

7. What do I think of when I go into a grocery store? _____

_____

_____

Follow-up

G. Dictation: Write the sentences that your teacher reads aloud.

1. _____

2. _____

3. _____

4. _____

5. _____

H. Listen to the definitions of words from the word form chart of this unit. Say each word that the teacher defines.

1. Hard to please.
2. Ready and wanting to.
3. Happening in a short time.
4. A person who sells foods and supplies.
5. A piece of paper or cloth that gives information.
6. A program for action.
7. A number of similar things or events coming one after another.
8. Coming at the end.
9. A thing used as a model.
10. A natural preference to act in a certain way.

I. Describe the grocery store that you go to.

Crime

Word Form Chart

NOUN	VERB	ADJECTIVE	ADVERB
alarm	alarm	alarmed	alarmingly
		alarming	
bribe	bribe	bribed	
bribery			
cell			
chase	chase	chased	
		chasing	
confession	confess	confessed	
		confessing	
conscience			
demand	demand	demanding	
denial	deny		
diamond			
doubt	doubt	doubtful	doubtfully
		doubting	undoubtedly
escape	escape	escaped	
		escaping	
fake	fake	fake	
guilt		guilty	guiltily
	hide (hid, hidden)	hidden	
		hiding	
identification	identify	identifying	
		identifiable	identifiably
incident			
innocence		innocent	innocently
jury			
juror			
pretense	pretend	pretending	
trap	trap	trapped	

Definitions and Examples

1. **guilty** [having done something wrong]

   The **guilty** man was sent to prison.
   The people who had seen the crime knew that she was **guilty** of it.

2. **guilt** [the bad feeling you get when you know that you have done something wrong]

   She was bothered by her **guilt** about stealing the money.

3. **innocent** [not having done anything wrong]

   The purpose of courts is to punish guilty people and protect
      innocent ones.
   It is terrible when an **innocent** person is sent to prison.

4. **jury** [a group of people who decide the guilt or innocence of a person in a court of law]

   The criminal was judged guilty by a **jury** of twelve men and
      women.
   The judge instructed the **jury** to listen carefully so that they could
      make a correct decision.

5. **cell** [a small, cage-like room for prisoners in a jail]

   The prisoner's **cell** was only six feet by eight feet.
   The jail is so crowded that there are at least three prisoners in each
      cell.

6. **escape** [to get away from the control of someone or something]

   The prisoner **escaped** from his cell during the night.
   His **escape** was successful; they could not find him.

7. **hide** (a) [to put yourself in a place where no one can see you]

   The escaped prisoner **hid** in the basement of the house.
   That criminal has been **hiding** from the police for years.

   (b) [to put something in a place where no one can see it]

   She **hid** the money so well that they never found it.

8. **diamond** [a precious white or clear stone]

   Diamonds are one of the hardest substances on earth; they can cut
      glass.
   She wore a **diamond** ring on her left hand.

9. **doubt** [to not believe completely; to not be sure of]

   I **doubt** that the stone is a diamond because it cost only ten dollars.
   The jury **doubted** the man's story and found him guilty.

10. **chase** [to follow someone or something in order to catch him or it]

    The police **chased** the escaped prisoner for ten miles before they
       caught him.
    The car **chase** in that movie was very exciting.

11. **deny** [to say that you did not do something]

    The prisoner **denied** that he had committed the murder.
    The police do not believe his **denial**; they believe that he is guilty.

12. **confess** [to say that you did something (usually something bad)]

    The prisoner **confessed** to committing the murder.
    The police had the man sign his written **confession**.

13. **conscience** [one's own feeling of what is right and wrong]

    Her guilty **conscience** made her confess to her crime.
    My **conscience** tells me how I should act.

14. **identify** [to determine exactly who someone is or what something is]

    The woman **identified** the stolen diamond as hers.
    The police asked us to **identify** the guilty person.
    In many countries, people must carry official **identification** cards.

15. **alarm** (a) [a warning sound or signal]

    The prison **alarm** sounded when they discovered the escape.
    If you hear the fire **alarm**, leave the building immediately.

    (b) [to frighten or worry]

    People in this neighborhood are **alarmed** by the recent increase in
       crime.

16. **bribe** [money, or something else of value, offered dishonestly or
    illegally to get some services]

    The criminal tried to **bribe** some members of the jury so that they
       would not find him guilty.
    Bribing a government official is a crime.
    He was sent to prison for **bribery**.

17. **demand** [to ask insistently for something that you think is owed to you]

> The thief **demanded** all the victims' money.
> The prisoners **demanded** to speak to the head officials at the prison.

18. **incident** [something that happens]

> There was an **incident** at the prison last night, two prisoners tried to escape.
> She feels very guilty about that **incident**.

19. **pretend** (a) [to give the idea that something is true when it is not]

> The guilty woman is **pretending** to be innocent.
> The prisoner escaped by **pretending** to be a guard.

   (b) [to imagine]

> Children like to **pretend** to be adults when they play.

20. **fake** [not real; not genuine]

> Her diamond ring looked genuine, but it was a **fake**.
> The criminal had a **fake** identity card.

21. **trap** [a device or a situation for catching an animal or a person]

> The police set up a **trap** on the road to catch the escaped prisoners.
> People sometimes catch animals in **traps**.

Introductory Exercises

A. Match each word with its definition.

_____ 1. not real; not genuine

_____ 2. having done something wrong

_____ 3. a precious stone

_____ 4. to get away from the control of someone

_____ 5. to not believe

_____ 6. to follow someone in order to catch him

_____ 7. to put yourself in a place so that no one can see you

_____ 8. a small cage-like room for prisoners in a jail

_____ 9. a device or a situation for catching an animal or person

_____ 10. to say that you did something bad

_____ 11. not having done anything wrong

_____ 12. to say that you did not do something

_____ 13. a group of people who decide the guilt or innocence of a person in a court of law

a. alarm
b. bribe
c. cell
d. chase
e. confess
f. conscience
g. demand
h. deny
i. diamond
j. doubt
k. escape
l. fake
m. guilty
n. hide
o. identify
p. incident
q. innocent
r. jury
s. pretend
t. trap

B. Answer each question with a word from the word form chart in this unit.

1. What do you use to catch someone?
2. What does a prisoner live in?
3. What is the money which a criminal may try to give to a juror?
4. What tells you that you have done something wrong?
5. When a habitual criminal denies committing a crime, what do people think?
6. What do the police use fingerprints for?
7. What rings at a bank during a robbery?
8. What is worth a lot of money?
9. What do children often do when they play?
10. Who makes the decisions in many courts?
11. What are the two possible decisions in a court?

Study Exercises

C. Match each word or phrase with its opposite.

    ____ **1.** innocent   **a.** confess

    ____ **2.** deny   **b.** doubt

                                         c. demand

    ____ **3.** genuine   **d.** fake

    ____ **4.** in sight   **e.** guilty

    ____ **5.** believe   **f.** hidden

                                         g. incident

D. In the blanks, write the appropriate word(s) from the word form chart in this unit.

1. That man gave a $1,000 _____ to the policeman who helped him escape.

2. The police think that she is guilty and _____ her story of her innocence.

3. Several police cars _____ the speeding car for ten miles, but they could not catch it.

4. The robbery victim _____ the jewelry which the police had found as hers.

5. That criminal must have no _____ ; he never feels guilty about any of his crimes.

6. A: What's that loud noise?

   B: Maybe it's some kind of _____ .

7. The police put the criminal in a small _____ .

8. The police wrote out the _____ which the man had made and then asked him to sign it.

9. I think that the painting is a _____ ; it does not look genuine.

10. The thief tried to _____ the stolen diamond, but the police easily found it.

E. Read the passage and answer the questions that follow.

DIAMOND THIEF CAUGHT

    At 1:30 this morning, local police finally caught the jewel thief whom they had been trying to trap for the past two months. Although the man they arrested, James Smith, denied that he was the thief, he was captured with several
5 diamond rings in his possession.

Police saw Smith leaving a jewelry store on Main Street at 1:16 A.M. On seeing the police, Smith jumped into his auto, and a high-speed chase followed for the next fourteen minutes. The police finally forced Smith off the road, and his
10 car hit a tree.

When the police searched Smith's clothing, they found the diamond rings hidden in an inside pocket of his jacket. Although Smith claimed that the diamonds were fake, the owner of the jewelry store where the most recent robbery
15 incident happened identified them as his missing jewels.

Smith is now awaiting his first visit to court in a cell in the town jail. If he does not confess, a jury will have to decide his guilt or innocence. However, a representative of the police stated today that they have no doubt that he will
20 be found to be guilty. This spokesman also stated that they hoped that the alarm caused in the community by all the recent robberies would be calmed by Smith's arrest.

1. How long had the police been looking for the thief? _____

_____

2. How did the police catch Smith? Was catching him easy? _____

_____

3. Where did Smith have the diamond rings? _____

_____

4. How did the police know that the diamond rings were the same

ones which were recently stolen? _____

_____

5. Do the police think that a jury will find Smith to be guilty? How

sure are they? _____

_____

6. How had the community felt during the period of the robberies? ___

_____

Follow-up

F.   Dictation: Write the sentences that your teacher reads aloud.

1. _____

2. _____

3. _____

4. _____

5. _____

G.   Answer the following questions.

1. Do the courts in your country use a jury system? If so, how many members does a jury have?
2. What kinds of alarms have you heard? What is the purpose of each alarm?
3. Do citizens in your country carry official identity cards? What is on the cards?
4. Have you ever seen the inside of a jail or prison? How big were the cells?
5. How do you know when your conscience is bothering you about something?
6. Can you tell a fake diamond from a real one? How?
7. What kinds of things are diamonds used for in your country? As jewelry, do they have any special meaning?
8. When you were a child, what did you like to pretend?
9. What incident was the most serious crime in your country during the past year?
10. Who may be bribed and why?

H.   Tell a story about the following:

Peter Brown is an innocent man, but he was sent to prison. He decides to escape . . .

Food

Word Form Chart

NOUN	VERB	ADJECTIVE	ADVERB
alcohol		alcoholic	
alcoholic			
alcoholism			
assembly	assemble	assembled	
assembler			
basket			
basketful			
		bitter	bitterly
brand	brand	branding	
		branded	
content(s)			
cream	cream	creamy	
		creamed	
dairy		dairy	
jar			
lamb			
nut		nuts	
		nutty	
	pour	pouring	
		raw	
shake	shake (shook, shaken)	shaking	
		shook	
swelling	swell (swelled, swollen)	swollen	
		swelling	
	stir	stirred	
		stirring	

NOUN	VERB	ADJECTIVE	ADVERB
toast	toast	toasted	
		toasting	
toaster			
tongue			
waste	waste	wasteful	wastefully
		wasted	

Definitions and Examples

1. **alcohol** [a liquid such as beer that can make you feel and act strangely]

    People under 20 or 21 years of age are not allowed to drink **alcohol** in some states.
    When people drink too much **alcohol**, they sometimes act foolishly.

2. **alcoholism** [a disease in which people drink too much alcohol and are not able to stop drinking]

    People who drink a lot of beer every day suffer from **alcoholism**.
    Special groups can help **alcoholics** to quit drinking.

3. **assemble** [to put or bring several things together in order to make something complete; to collect]

    The cook **assembled** several things she needed to make a cake: eggs, milk, and sugar.
    It is possible to buy a bicycle that you **assemble** yourself, and it is cheaper! It is more expensive to buy a bicycle already **assembled** at the store.

4. **assembly** [a meeting of a large group of people to listen to a special speech or program, usually in a school]

    Our high school has an **assembly** every two weeks.
    There was an **assembly** yesterday evening of students interested in studying medicine.

5. **basket** [a container usually made of plant material]

    My grandmother picks flowers from her garden and puts them in a **basket**.
    Women used to go shopping at a market and put their food in a **basket**, but today people shop at grocery stores and put their food in paper bags.

6. **bitter** (a) [a sharp, unpleasant taste]

   Some unripe fruit has a **bitter** flavor.

   A: I don't like this drink. It's very **bitter**.
   B: Put some sugar in it.

   (b) [full of hate]

   People who have had a hard life often become **bitter** when they are older.
   Couples who fight a lot sometimes have **bitter** divorces.

7. **brand** (a) [a group of products made by the same manufacturer; the name of a group of products]

   Some **brands** of shoes are better than others; they are stronger and last longer.

   A: What **brand** of toothpaste do you use?
   B: I use the **brand** in the red and blue box.

   (b) [a mark of ownership burned on the skin of cattle]

   For one hundred years, cattle from different ranches all lived together in the same fields, so farmers **branded** their cattle in order to identify them.
   The **brand** for Mr. Jones' cattle is a J in a circle: ⨍

8. **contents** (usually plural) [anything inside a container or in a book, speech, etc.]

   The circus clown showed the audience a box, but the **contents** of the box were a secret.

   Immigration officer: What are the **contents** of these bags?
   Tourist: Only some presents for my family.

9. **nut** (a) [a dry fruit or seed with a hard outer cover]

   Birds are able to break the outside of some **nuts** and eat the soft part inside.
   I love to eat **nuts** while I watch TV.

   (b) {informal} [a person who likes to have fun; a crazy person]

   My uncle is a **nut**—he is 50 years old and still plays like a child.
   You are **nuts** if you think that I want to go camping in 0° F weather!

10. **stir** [to move a spoon or a stick around in something]

    The man put milk and sugar in his coffee and **stirred** it with a spoon.
    For the party, I made a special dish. I put several kinds of nuts in a bowl and **stirred** them together with salt and special flavors.

11. **cream** (a) [the part of milk that contains fat]

> Good restaurants serve **cream** with coffee instead of milk.
> I love baked foods made with **cream**, but they are very fattening.

(b) [to beat or stir until smooth and soft]

> To make a cake, you must first **cream** butter and eggs together.
> The cook **creamed** three sticks of butter before he added **cream** and sugar.

(c) [a liquid that looks like cream, often used as medicine or to put on the body]

> If your hands are very dry in the winter, you should use hand **cream** to keep them soft.
> Doctors recommend putting a medicinal **cream** on a cut to prevent infection.

12. **dairy** (a) [a farm that produces milk and milk products]

> My grandparents have a **dairy** with 500 cows.

(b) [a business that makes butter, cheese, and other products from milk]

> The butter and cream from our neighborhood **dairy** are better than nationally famous brands.
> In the grocery store you can find eggs in the **dairy** section.

13. **jar** [a container with a wide mouth (opening), usually made of glass]

> The child cut his finger when he broke the glass **jar** of candy.
> Be careful when you put a lid on a **jar**; sometimes **jars** break.
>
> A: Do you want something from the store?
> B: Yes. Please bring me a **jar** of coffee.

14. **lamb** (a) [a young or baby sheep]

> On my grandfather's farm, three **lambs** were born this spring.

(b) [the meat from baby sheep]

> I love to eat **lamb**, but it is an expensive meat in the United States.

15. **pour** (a) [to cause something to flow, usually from a container]

> John **poured** a glass of beer for each of his friends, but he forgot to **pour** one for himself.
> I always keep sugar in a glass jar, so when I buy sugar, I **pour** it from the bag into a glass jar.

(b) [to rain very hard]

> It looks as if it is going to **pour**.
>
> A: How was your vacation?
> B: It was good, but it **poured** the entire two weeks.

16. **raw** [not cooked; in a natural state]

> For my lunch I always eat a sandwich and **raw** vegetables.
> "Kibbee" is the name of an Arabic dish made from **raw** lamb, and
>   "ceviche" is a Latin American dish made with **raw** fish.
> Iron and wood are important **raw** materials.

17. **shake** (a) [to move something quickly up and down]

> You should **shake** a bottle of medicine in order to stir the contents.
> Children like to **shake** things that make a loud noise.
> To make a **milkshake**, put milk and ice cream in a container and
>   **shake** them together until they are combined.

    (b) [to take someone else's hand]

> Americans usually **shake** hands when they meet for the first time.
> Friends do not **shake** hands every time they meet, only when
>   they have not seen each other for a long time.
> Businessmen **shake** hands when they agree to do business together.

18. **swell** [to get bigger; to increase in size]

> Rice **swells** as it cooks.
> My toe **swelled** when I dropped a jar on it.

19. **swelling** [something that is swollen]

> The **swelling** on my head is a result of my car accident last week.

20. **toast** (a) [to heat a food, usually bread, until it is brown]

> I prefer to **toast** my bread when I make a sandwich.

> A: Do you want **toast** or bread for breakfast?
> B: I'd like **toast**, please.

    (b) [to warm completely]

> The children **toasted** their feet by the fire.
> We were freezing from the snow, so we **toasted** ourselves in front of
>   the heater for a half hour.

21. **toaster** [a small machine for making toast]

> He put the bread in the **toaster**.

22. **tongue** [the part inside the mouth that moves and is used to help in speaking and eating]

> I bit my **tongue** last night while I was eating dinner, and it still
>   hurts.
> Americans do not eat much **tongue**, but in some countries beef
>   **tongue** is a very special food.

23.   **waste** [to spend or use foolishly]

> To spend a lot of money on an old car is a **waste** of money.
>
> Mother: Don't **waste** your time watching so much TV.
> Child: But I like TV.
> Mother: I know you do. But it is a **waste** of time because the programs are so stupid. Read a book instead.

Introductory Exercises

A.   Match each word with its definition.

____ 1. uncooked

____ 2. what is inside a container

____ 3. to increase in size

____ 4. to bring several things together

____ 5. to heat food until it is brown

____ 6. an unpleasant flavor

____ 7. a container made of glass

____ 8. the part inside your mouth that moves

____ 9. the name of a group of products

____ 10. meat from a baby sheep

____ 11. the fat part of milk

____ 12. to move something quickly up and down

____ 13. a farm that produces milk and milk products

    a. alcohol
    b. assemble
    c. basket
    d. bitter
    e. brand
    f. contents
    g. cream
    h. dairy
    i. jar
    j. lamb
    k. nut
    l. pour
    m. raw
    n. shake
    o. swell
    p. stir
    q. toast
    r. tongue
    s. waste

B.   Answer **TRUE** or **FALSE**.

1. A person who is an alcoholic should not drink beer.
2. A basket is usually made from metal.
3. A glass jar will break if you drop it.
4. Cream rises to the top of milk.
5. You should stir tea with a fork.
6. Wood swells if it gets wet.
7. Clothes made of cotton swell if they are washed in hot water.

8. Cakes usually have a bitter flavor.
9. People never eat raw vegetables.
10. You can put cream in tea.
11. A lamb is a cow's baby.
12. Toast is made by boiling nuts.
13. Students play football at an assembly.
14. It is not a waste to eat half of a sandwich and throw the other part away.

Study Exercises

C. In the blanks, write the appropriate word(s) from the word form chart in this unit.

1. John lost his job after the strike, and he now is _____ about his company and the union.

2. I can't eat this meat—it's still _____ . I think our oven isn't working correctly.

3. Most _____ are born in the spring.

4. After I go swimming, I always put _____ on my arms and legs to prevent them from becoming too dry.

5. Without our lips, teeth, and _____ , humans couldn't eat or talk.

6. The important world leaders _____ hands when they met at the International Peace Ceremony.

7. Jane was surprised at the _____ of the package she received from her boyfriend. It contained a diamond ring!

8. My boss is _____ . First, she asks me to do one thing, and then five minutes later she asks me to do the opposite!

9. We always send our mother a _____ full of flowers for her birthday.

10. Jim made too much rice for dinner last night. He forgot how much rice _____ when it cooks.

11. The child dropped the milk bottle while he _____ a glass of milk for himself.

12. I went to the grocery store this morning to buy some soap, but the store didn't have the _____ I usually use.

13. Could you please _____ the soup that's on the stove? My hands are covered with soap.

D. Match each word with its opposite.

        ____ **1.** bitter   **a.** shrink

        ____ **2.** swell   **b.** burned

        ____ **3.** assemble   **c.** fill

        ____ **4.** waste   **d.** ranch

        ____ **5.** toast   **e.** freeze

        ____ **6.** raw   **f.** separate

                                  g. intelligent

                                  h. sweet

                                  i. save

E. Fill in the blanks with a word from the word form chart in this unit. You may use words more than once.

It's almost Christmas time now, and my family is preparing for our annual celebration. Christmas is my favorite holiday, so I like to do a lot of different things to celebrate. I especially like to make some of the foods that are traditional at this time of year. The first food is a drink called "Wassail" which comes from England. Wassail is made from cream and several different kinds of (1) _____ , including beer. You (2) _____ these all together in a large jar and then (3) _____ the (4) _____ well. We always serve Wassail at our annual Christmas party.

I also make a special Christmas cake for our party. To make the cake, you need cream, eggs, butter, dried fruit, and alcohol. First, let the fruit sit in the alcohol until it's (5) _____ . The cream and butter should be fresh; the (6) _____ of these is not important but you should get the freshest ones that are in the (7) _____ section of the supermarket. Stir everything together, even the alcohol from the dried fruit. Don't waste anything! Put a little sugar on the top, and bake it for 45 minutes.

During the Christmas season, we put lots of lights around the outside of the house. We also put baskets around the inside of the house. The (8) _____ of the (9) _____ are different — some have candy, some have nuts, and some have Christmas flowers. We spend about two weeks preparing for the Christmas holidays. Some of our friends think we are (10) _____ to spend so much time and effort, but it's worth it when the whole family (11) _____ on Christmas morning.

Follow-up

F.   Dictation: Write the sentences that your teacher reads aloud.

1. _____

2. _____

3. _____

4. _____

5. _____

G.   Answer the following questions.

1. Name some foods that taste bitter.
2. Name some foods or drinks that you can pour.
3. What are some things you can use a basket for?
4. What brand of coffee do you like best?
5. What do you put cream on in your country? Or what have you had with cream in this country?
6. What do you think is a waste of money?
   What do you think is a waste of time?
7. How do you make a milkshake?
8. What kind of alcohol do people in your country drink?
9. Do people brand cattle and sheep in your country? If not, how do they identify their animals?
10. Describe the contents of your purse or backpack.
11. Do you eat lamb for any special holidays? If not, what meat do you eat?
12. What do you do if your foot or hand swells?
13. What food do you eat toasted?
14. What foods can you buy in jars?

H.   Tell how to make a dish from your country. Use words from this unit.

Military

Word Form Chart

NOUN	VERB	ADJECTIVE	ADVERB	PREPOSITION
board				
concern	concern	concerned		concerning
		considerable	considerably	
courage		courageous	courageously	
event		eventful	eventfully	
gain	gain	gaining		
		gained		
general				
giant		giant		
		great	greatly	
knot	knot	knotted		
lieutenant				
memorial	memorialize	memorialized		
memory	memorize	memorized		
obedience	obey	obedient	obediently	
disobedience	disobey	disobedient	disobediently	
occurrence	occur	occurring		
operation	operate	operating		
private				
rope	rope	roped		
situation	situate	situated		
stupidity		stupid	stupidly	
target	target	targeted		

Definitions and Examples

1. **giant** [very large]

    Some of the navy's **giant** ships carry fighter planes.
    One form of air travel is in **giant** balloons.

2. **general** [the highest officer's rank in an army]

    Usually the army of a country will have only a few **generals**.
    He was promoted to the rank of **general** when he was 50 years old.

3. **private** (a) [the lowest rank in an army]

    Privates do not give orders; they only follow orders.
    Most people in the army are **privates**.

    (b) [2-1: Not open to all people]

    Only invited people attended the **private** meeting.

4. **lieutenant** [the lowest officer's rank in an army]

    My brother is a **lieutenant**, but he hopes to be promoted to captain
    soon.
    The **lieutenant** ordered the privates to begin digging holes to
    hide in.

5. **memorial** [something which helps us remember an important time,
    person, etc.]

    There is a large Vietnam War **memorial** in Washington, D.C.
    A **memorial** meeting was held by the relatives of the soldiers who
    had died.

6. **memorize** [to remember something very exactly]

    Students learning a second language must **memorize** many words.

7. **memory** (a) [the ability to remember]

    He has a good **memory**; he can remember things that he has only
    heard or seen once.

    (b) [something which you remember]

    A: Do you have good or bad **memories** of your childhood?
    B: Most of my **memories** are good ones.

8. **considerable** [a lot of]

> **Considerable** experience is required to become a general in the army.
>
> For most people, it takes **considerable** effort to memorize a long poem.

9. **occur** [to happen]

> That battle **occurred** near the beginning of the war.
>
> Most people would like to prevent the **occurrence** of wars.

10. **event** [an important happening or incident]

> The **event** which brought the United States into World War II was the bombing of Pearl Harbor in Hawaii.
>
> Countries often have national holidays to celebrate important **events** in their histories.
>
> You can read about current **events** in the newspaper.

11. **courage** [bravery]

> That soldier has a lot of **courage**; he risked his own life to save two other soldiers.
>
> The **courageous** lieutenant led his men into battle.

12. **rope** [a long thin piece of material]

> **Rope** is thicker than string.
>
> The sailors used **ropes** to lower the small boats into the water.
>
> He put a **rope** around the horse's neck to lead it.

13. **knot** [something which you tie in a rope or a string]

> He tied a **knot** with the two ropes to make one long rope.
>
> A: How many kinds of **knots** can you tie?
> B: Not many.

14. **stupid** [not intelligent]

> Many people feel that all wars are **stupid**.
>
> The **stupid** soldier shot himself in the foot by accident.

15. **obey** [to do what someone in authority tells you to do]

> Soldiers must **obey** their orders.
> You should **obey** the traffic laws when you drive.
> Parents like their children to be **obedient**.

16. **concern** (a) [a worry]

   The families of soldiers always feel **concern** about them during
      wars.
   The lieutenant was **concerned** that his men were too tired and
      hungry to fight.

   (b) [to be about; to be connected with]

   That soldier's job is **concerned** with repairing bombers.

17. **target** (a) [something you are shooting at]

   The bombers' **target** was a weapons factory.
   The soldier hit his **target** and saw the man fall.

   b) [something you want to reach or get]

   Our company's **target** is to double our sales.

18. **gain** [to get; to reach]

   After six hours of fighting, the army had **gained** about half a mile of
      ground.
   The lieutenant **gained** the respect of his men by his courageous
      actions.

19. **board** [a flat piece of wood]

   The soldier tied the **boards** together to form a ladder.
   The little bridge was made of wooden **boards**.

20. **great** [very important, or very big]

   World War I was called the **Great** War until World War II.
   Many people feel that President Kennedy was a **great** leader.

21. **situation** [the state or condition]

   That country's **situation** is very dangerous; its neighbor has a large
      army and is threatening to attack.
   A general must be able to look at a military **situation** and make
      decisions about it.

22. **operation** (a) [a procedure including planning and action]

   The generals are planning an **operation** that should take two days
      and help end the war soon.
   The **operation** was successful, and they defeated their enemy.

   (b) [medical repair of the body by a doctor]

   The man had an **operation** to repair his heart.
   An **operation** is usually done in a hospital.

Introductory Exercises

A. Match each word with its definition.

_____ 1. the lowest rank in an army

_____ 2. something which helps us
remember an important time,
person, etc.

_____ 3. a lot of

_____ 4. bravery

_____ 5. not intelligent

_____ 6. something you shoot at

_____ 7. very important, or big

_____ 8. very large

_____ 9. the lowest officer's rank in
an army

_____ 10. to happen

_____ 11. to do what someone in authority
tells you to do

_____ 12. to get or to reach

_____ 13. the highest officer's rank
in an army

_____ 14. an important happening or
incident

_____ 15. worry

_____ 16. a flat piece of wood

a. board
b. concern
c. considerable
d. courage
e. event
f. gain
g. general
h. giant
i. great
j. knot
k. lieutenant
l. memorial
m. obey
n. occur
o. operation
p. private
q. rope
r. situation
s. stupid
t. target

B. Answer each question with a word from the word form chart in this
unit.

1. What do soldiers do when they receive orders?
2. What is a very big person?
3. What do people shoot guns at?
4. What can you make with a rope?
5. What can you use to build a house?
6. What is someone who is brave in the face of danger?
7. Name three ranks in an army.

Study Exercises

C. Match each word with its synonym.

_____ 1. concern
_____ 2. considerable
_____ 3. courageous
_____ 4. event
_____ 5. memory
_____ 6. occur
_____ 7. situation
_____ 8. stupid

a. much
b. happen
c. unintelligent
d. brave
e. worry
f. condition
g. remembrance
h. incident

D. Match each word with its opposite.

_____ 1. considerable
_____ 2. gain
_____ 3. giant
_____ 4. great
_____ 5. memorize
_____ 6. obey
_____ 7. stupid

a. tiny
b. smart
c. little
d. forget
e. disobey
f. lose
g. unimportant

E. In the blanks, write the appropriate word(s) from the word form chart in this unit.

1. Soldiers get into trouble if they do not _____ their orders.

2. The lieutenant _____ the respect of his men because of his courage.

3. The _____ battle lasted for three days and caused the death of thousands of soldiers.

4. The lieutenant was responsible for some of the plans, but the general was in command of the whole _____ .

5. She tied the boards together with a _____ .

6. The soldiers had to _____ their instructions; they were not allowed to write them down.

7. Of the ten shots, only one hit the _____ ; he was not a good shot.

8. The event _____ two weeks ago. Since then I have not been able to forget it.

9. There is no need for _____ . Our forces are winning the battle and have suffered few losses.

10. After _____ training, the soldiers were able to operate the new weapons efficiently.

F. Read the passage and answer the questions that follow.

Today the military announced the conclusion of its "war games" which have been occurring during the past three weeks in the mountainous region surrounding the small town of Hicksburg. While pleased that the military operation
5 in their backyard is over for this year, the townspeople are continuing their argument with the military concerning the necessity of the yearly "war games."

Spokesmen for the military insist that such giant yearly operations are needed to make sure that the soldiers have
10 gained the fighting skills required for battle. They state that only by experiencing a battlelike situation can these skills be tested. Spokesmen emphasized that in addition to measuring battle skills such as hitting targets and memorizing maps, the games give the officers a chance to test the obedience and
15 courage of their men.

The townspeople reply that the games cause them considerable inconvenience each year. They insist that it is stupid to invent a warlike situation and that the yearly event usually results in injuries to some of the soldiers. The
20 townspeople are requesting that if the yearly games must occur, the event be moved to a different location each year.

1. How long did the "war games" last? _____
_____

2. What do the townspeople disagree with the military about? _____
_____

3. Why does the military feel that the "war games" are needed? _____
_____

4. What are two examples of battle skills? _____
_____
_____

5. What two other characteristics of their men can the officers see during the games? _____

_____

_____

6. Why do the townpeople call the games stupid? _____

_____

Follow-up

G. Dictation: Write the sentences that your teacher reads aloud.

1. _____

2. _____

3. _____

4. _____

5. _____

H. Answer the following questions.

1. What current situation are you concerned about?
2. What was the most important event in your country in the past five years?
3. How do you think an army officer can gain the respect of his men?
4. Are there any war memorials in your country? Explain.
5. Should a soldier always obey his orders? Why or why not?
6. Name something that you have a considerable amount of.
7. Describe a courageous act which you have seen.
8. Who do you think is the greatest person in the history of your country?
9. Do you have a special method for memorizing vocabulary? Explain.
10. Have you ever climbed a rope? Why? How high?

I. Explain the advantages and disadvantages of being . . .

1) a private
2) a general

Family

Word Form Chart

NOUN	VERB	ADJECTIVE	ADVERB
	accompany	accompanying accompanied	
ancestor bachelor bachelorhood		ancestral	
	bring up (brought up, brought up) care about care for		
companion companionship			
delight	delight	delightful delighted	delightfully delightedly
discouragement	discourage	discouraging discouraged elder	discouragingly
elderly encouragement	encourage	elderly encouraging encouraged	encouragingly
generation orphan orphanage	orphan		
permission	permit	permitted	
pet	pet		
selfishness unselfishness		selfish unselfish	selfishly unselfishly
surroundings	surround	surrounding surrounded	
widow widower	widow	widowed	

Definitions and Examples

1. **bachelor** [a man who has not married]

   My uncle was a **bachelor** until age 40, when he got married.
   She wants to find a nice **bachelor** to marry.

2. **pet** [an animal which is kept to be a friend]

   Many Americans have dogs and cats for **pets**.
   My apartment lease says, "No **pets** allowed."

3. **widow** [a woman whose husband has died]

   The woman who lives next door is a **widow**.
   She was **widowed** five years ago when her husband died of a heart
     attack.

4. **widower** [a man whose wife has died]

   My friend married a **widower** whose wife had died two years ago.
   There always seem to be more widows than **widowers**.

5. **generation** [a group of people born and living at about the same time]

   You are the same **generation** as your cousins, but a different
     generation from your aunts and uncles.
   Today's **generation** has many advantages that **generations** in the
     past did not have.

6. **ancestor** [one's relative in the past, now dead]

   One of her **ancestors** established this town more than one hundred
     years ago.
   My **ancestors** came to this country many generations ago.

7. **elderly** [old (used only for people)]

   My grandmother is quite **elderly** now.
   The **elderly** man was losing his hearing.
   Young people should help the **elderly**.

8. **companion** [a friend; someone who is often with another person]

   On a long journey, it is good to have traveling **companions**.
   A dog or cat is often a **companion** to its owner.

9. **accompany** [to go with]

> I **accompanied** my elderly grandmother on her vacation. She needed a companion to help her travel.

10. **permission** [agreement from a person in authority to let someone do or have something]

> My parents gave me **permission** to stay out until midnight.
> We need to get **permission** to take the exam on a different day because of our trip.

11. **delightful** [very pleasing]

> That was a **delightful** day. I had a very nice time.
> She was **delighted** with her good grades.

12. **encourage** [to give hope or courage to]

> My parents **encouraged** me in my studies.
> Most children need **encouragement** to learn to play a musical instrument.

13. **discourage** [to cause to lose hope or enthusiasm]

> The child was **discouraged** by his bad grades and did not want to go to school.
> The constant rain during our vacation at the beach **discouraged** us.

14. **selfish** [concerned about oneself; without thinking of others]

> The **selfish** child would not share his toys with his brother.
> No one likes a **selfish** person.
> Jane is always **unselfish** with her money; she gives a lot to people who need it.

15. **surroundings** [the environment; the people and things in the area around someone or something]

> This is a nice apartment, but the **surroundings** are not very nice.
> The neighborhood really needs some improvements.
> The area which **surrounds** the campus is beautiful.
>
> A: What kind of **surroundings** do you prefer?
> B: Quiet ones.

16. **bring up** (a) {separable} [to raise (children)]

   He was **brought up** by his grandparents after his parents died.
   He was three when his parents were killed. His grandparents
      brought him **up** after that.

   (b) {separable} [to introduce a topic, question, etc.]

   A: Who **brought up** the topic of money?
   B: I did.

17. **care about** [to think something or someone is important; to love]

   If you **care about** your health, you should eat good meals.
   He does not **care about** his grades, so he is failing two courses.
   The person he **cares about** most is his son.

18. **care for** (a) [to provide necessary services for]

   He **cared for** his sick mother 24 hours a day.
   She **cares for** her younger sisters while her parents are at work.

   (b) [to like; to love]

   They **care** very much **for** each other and are planning to get married
      soon.

   A: Would you **care for** some tea?
   B: Yes. Thank you.

19. **orphan** [a child whose parents have died]

   Some **orphans** live in **orphanages** run by the government.
   Those children were **orphaned** at a young age.

Introductory Exercises

A. Match each word with its definition.

_____ 1. a woman whose husband has died

_____ 2. agreement to let someone have or do something

_____ 3. to think someone or something is important

_____ 4. very pleasing

_____ 5. to go with

_____ 6. an animal which is kept to be a friend

_____ 7. a man who has not married

_____ 8. to raise

_____ 9. to give hope or courage to

_____ 10. concerned about oneself; without thinking of others

_____ 11. to provide necessary services for

_____ 12. to cause to lose hope or enthusiasm

_____ 13. old

_____ 14. a group of people born and living at about the same time

_____ 15. one's relative in the past, now dead

_____ 16. someone who is often with another person

a. accompany
b. ancestor
c. bachelor
d. bring up
e. care about
f. care for
g. companion
h. delightful
i. discourage
j. elderly
k. encourage
l. generation
m. permission
n. pet
o. selfish
p. surrounding
q. widow

B. Answer each question with a word from the word form chart in this unit.

1. What is a cat which lives in a person's house?
2. How do you feel when you study hard but still fail a test?
3. What do you call a child who will not share his toys?
4. What is a man who has not married?
5. What does a child need to stay up late?
6. What is a man whose wife has died?
7. What are you when you are very happy about something?

    8. What is all around you?
    9. What do parents do to their children? (three answers)
  10. What is a person who goes somewhere with another person?

Study Exercises

C.   Write **T** if the sentence is true and **F** if it is false.

    ____   **1.** Your ancestors are younger than you are.

    ____   **2.** Parents are delighted when their children are selfish.

    ____   **3.** A pet may live in a person's home.

    ____   **4.** Parents should encourage their children to study.

    ____   **5.** Failure can cause a person to become discouraged.

    ____   **6.** Your mother might be a bachelor.

    ____   **7.** You are a member of the same generation as your grandmother.

    ____   **8.** Parents often accompany their small children on vacation.

    ____   **9.** Children should ask their parents for permission before they stay out late at night.

  ____ **10.** A young person can be elderly.

D.   In the blanks, write the appropriate word(s) from the word form chart in this unit.

    1. John wanted to go camping with some older boys, but his parents would not give him _____ .

    2. My _____ settled in this town one hundred years ago, and my family has lived here ever since.

    3. I am _____ my brother's pets while he is on vacation. I have to feed them twice a day.

    4. My grandmother is quite _____ . She is almost 90 years old.

    5. My aunt was _____ three years ago when her husband died of cancer.

    6. Most people want to _____ their children to be like themselves.

    7. Each year after the long winter, we are _____ when the beautiful spring weather arrives.

8. Her parents are _____ her to finish her college before she gets married. They are very much in favor of education.

9. Who will _____ the children on their trip to the museum this afternoon?

10. My father got very _____ when he lost his job.

11. Whenever John wanted a _____ to travel with him, he invited Bill.

E.   Read the passage and answer the questions that follow.

The United States has been criticized for its treatment of its elderly citizens. Although in many other countries the elderly usually live with their children's family, many older Americans live alone, without the close companionship of
5   their children. This situation is sometimes blamed on the "selfishness" of the younger generation, but a closer look reveals that many of the elderly prefer to maintain their independent lives.
    Research on the situation of the elderly in America has
10 shown that while grandparents are delighted to be visited periodically by their children and grandchildren, they prefer to continue living in the surroundings that they are familiar with. This suggests that children should permit their parents to live alone if they wish to, but should encourage them to
15 maintain close ties to the rest of the family.
    Another surprising result of research on the elderly in the United States has been the very positive influence which pets have been found to have on the older people that they live with. It has been shown that elderly people who care for
20 small pets, such as cats and dogs, live longer, are healthier, and have better attitudes towards their lives than similar older people without these companions.

1. How do many elderly Americans live? _____

_____

2. What do some people see as the cause of this situation? _____

_____

3. Where do many of the elderly want to live? _____

_____

4. What kind of influence do pets have on the elderly? _____

_____

5. What can be the result for an older person of owning a cat? (three things)

a) _____

b) _____

c) _____

Follow-up

F. Dictation: Write the sentences that your teacher reads aloud.

1. _____

2. _____

3. _____

4. _____

5. _____

G. Answer the following questions.

1. Does anyone accompany you to school each day? Who?
2. Where did your ancestors live 100 years ago? Two hundred years ago?
3. What percent of the men in your country are bachelors after age 40?
4. Who usually brings up orphans in your country?
5. Who is the most elderly person in your family? How old is he/she?
6. Do people in your country commonly have pets? What kind?
7. For what kinds of things do sixteen-year-olds need permission from their parents in your country?
8. Do widows in your country often remarry? Why or why not?
9. What kind of surroundings do you like best?
10. What kinds of actions are thought to be selfish in your country?
11. Who are your favorite companions?

H. Describe a time when you were very discouraged or a time when you were very encouraged.

Nature

Word Form Chart

NOUN	VERB	ADJECTIVE	ADVERB
bank			
bay			
creation	create	creative	creatively
creativity		created	
	feed (on)	feeding	
gathering	gather	gathering	
		gathered	
nest	nest	nesting	
organization	organize	organized	
organizer		organizing	
pink		pink	
		previous	previously
	remain	remaining	
replacement	replace	replaced	
rescue	rescue	rescued	
		rough	roughly
shell			
spill	spill	spilled	
star		starry	
stick			
wing		winged	

Definitions and Examples

1. **bank** (a) [the land along the side(s) of a river]

   Many animals live on the **banks** of a river.
   People often fish from the **banks** of a river.

   (b) [assumed: a business that handles money]

   I borrowed $10,000 from the **bank**.

2. **feed** (on) [to eat something in order to live]

   Large fish usually **feed on** smaller fish.

   A: What kind of food do birds eat?
   B: They **feed on** insects.

3. **gather** [to collect; to bring together from different places]

   The campers **gathered** wood for the fire.

   A: How do young birds get food?
   B: The adult birds **gather** insects and bring them to the young
   birds.

4. **stick** (a) [a small part of a tree that is broken off]

   We found many **sticks** on the ground after the storm.
   The little boy threw a **stick** for the dog to chase.

   (b) [3-5: to put something in place and make it stay there]

   Stick a stamp on the envelope.

5. **nest** [a home that a bird makes from sticks, grass, etc.
   to shelter its eggs and young]

   Young birds cannot leave their **nests** until they learn to fly.

   A: How do birds usually build their **nests**?
   B: They usually gather small sticks, grass, and feathers and take
   them to a high place where they build the **nest**.

6. **wing** [the part of a bird used for flying]

   Young birds must learn how to use their **wings** to fly.
   Airplanes have **wings**, but helicopters do not.

7. **create** [to bring something into existence; to make something]

   The birds **created** a nest from sticks and grass.
   That artist is very **creative**; he paints in ways that others have
   never thought of.

8. **pink** [a light reddish color]

> Most birds are **pink** at birth.
>
> A: Did you see the sunset last night?
> B: Yes, the sky was gold, blue, and **pink**.

9. **star** [any bright heavenly body; a tiny shining light seen in the night sky]

> We were able to see many **stars** last night because the sky was clear.
> The sun is a **star**.

10. **organize** [to give a shape or pattern to something]

> Zoos sometimes **organize** classes to teach children about animals.
> The purpose of that **organization** is the protection of animals in the wild.

11. **previously** [before something else]

> The ground was so dry that it was difficult to see where the stream had been **previously**.
> The land where the new buildings were constructed was **previously** a park.

12. **remain** [to stay in a place]

> Young birds must **remain** in their nests until they learn to fly.
> Mother birds **remain** close to their nests to protect their young.

13. **replace** [to substitute for; to put something back where it came from]

> Adult birds must **replace** sticks that fall from the nest.
> We need a new car to **replace** our old one.

14. **shell** [a thin, hard outer covering of some animals, animal eggs, or a seed of a plant]

> The **shells** of some animals provide protection against other animals.
>
> A: How are young birds born?
> B: They are born when they break out of the **shell** of the egg laid by their mother.

15. **rough** (a) [not smooth]

   A: The water in the lake was very **rough** yesterday.
   B: I know. I tried to go swimming, but the waves were too high.

   (b) [not gentle]

   Young animals often play **roughly** with one another.

16. **bay** [an area of water, on the coast, surrounded by land on most sides]

   The water in a **bay** is usually not as rough as in the ocean.
   Baltimore is on the Chesapeake **Bay**.

17. **rescue** [to save from danger]

   The child **rescued** the young bird when it fell from its nest.

   A: Yesterday I saw a large bird attack the nest of another bird.
   B: What happened? Was the mother bird able to **rescue** its baby?
   A: Yes, the mother **rescued** her baby by frightening the attacking bird.

18. **spill** [to cause or allow something to fall out of its container]

   During a flood, the water from a river flows over its banks and **spills** onto the land around it.

   A: Do you know what happened when my younger brother tried to put bird feed into the bird feeder?
   B: No, what happened?
   A: He fell, and the birdseed **spilled** all over the ground.

Introductory Exercises

A. Match each word with its definition.

____	1. to bring together from different places	**a.**	bank
____	2. to allow something to fall out of a container	**b.**	bay
____	3. to give shape to something	**c.**	create
____	4. a shining light seen in the night sky	**d.**	gather
____	5. to stay in a place	**e.**	nest
____	6. a small part of a tree that is broken off	**f.**	organize
____	7. to save from danger	**g.**	pink
____	8. the land along the sides of a river	**h.**	previous
____	9. a light reddish color	**i.**	remain
____	10. the part of a bird used for flying	**j.**	replace
____	11. to make something	**k.**	rescue
____	12. before something else	**l.**	rough
____	13. the home that a bird makes from sticks, grass, etc., to shelter its eggs and young	**m.**	shell
		n.	spill
		o.	star
		p.	stick
		q.	wing

B. Choose the word that best fits in the blank.

1. Young birds cannot leave their _____ until they learn to fly.

   a. wings   b. nest   c. shell

2. The children gathered many _____ to make a fire.

   a. sticks   b. bank   c. stars

3. The _____ of an egg provides protection for it.

   a. stick   b. wing   c. shell

4. Birds must _____ sticks and grass to make a good nest.

   a. bay   b. organize   c. create

5. Many people go fishing in a _____ .

   a. bank   b. bay   c. star

6. Large fish usually _____ small fish.

   a. feed on   b. gather   c. organize

7. The _____ of parks in cities is important, so that people can have a natural place for relaxation.

   a. removal   b. creation   c. remaining

8. The colors of the sunset are red, gold, and _____ .

   a. pink   b. shell   c. star

9. Young animals must _____ with their mothers until they can find food by themselves.

   a. nest   b. remain   c. feed on

10. It is dangerous to swim in _____ water.

    a. shell   b. rough   c. stick

Study Exercises

C. Write **T** if the sentence is true and **F** if it is false.

____ **1.** Birds have shells.

____ **2.** You can see many stars during the day.

____ **3.** People may sail their boats in bays.

____ **4.** Young children should swim in rough water.

____ **5.** Some animals sleep on the banks of a river.

____ **6.** Stars are pink.

____ **7.** Birds use sticks to build their nests.

____ **8.** Before you build something you must organize the things you need to build it.

____ **9.** Big fish feed on small fish.

____ **10.** Sometimes chemicals from a factory spill into a river.

D. In the blanks, write the appropriate word(s) from the word form chart in this unit.

1. Birds sit on their eggs in a _____ .

2. Many animals must _____ grass and _____ to build homes for their young.

3. Birds _____ insects.

4. Mother birds _____ close to their young.

5. If a young animal is in danger, its mother will try to _____ it.

6. Sometimes young animals play _____ with one another.

7. A young bird must learn to use its _____ -s in order to fly.

8. When a river overflows, it _____ onto the land around it.

9. Many people like to sit on the _____ of a river to relax.

10. The water in a _____ is usually not as rough as the water in the ocean.

11. Many animals must _____ their homes from their environment.

E.   Circle the word or phrase which is different in meaning.

1. remain   go   stay
2. home   nest   shell
3. food   stick   tree
4. eat   feed on   gather
5. banks   legs   wings
6. rescue   before   previously
7. replace   put back   remain
8. star   stick   sun
9. pink   shell   blue

F.   Read the passage and answer the questions that follow.

   Many kinds of birds must build nests for their young every year. First, they gather sticks and grass. Then they must organize the sticks and grass to create a good nest. Usually, the nest is rough, and the mother bird must find
5 soft feathers and grass to put in the nest.
   Baby birds are usually pink when they are born, and they do not have any feathers. They must remain in the nest until they learn to use their wings to fly. The mother is very busy during that time. Since birds feed on insects, the mother
10 brings many insects to her young. If they fall out of the nest, the mother bird must rescue them. Sometimes, the sticks and grass in the nest also fall out and must be replaced with new ones.

15 When the young birds are older, they do not depend on their mother as much as they did previously. At that time, they learn to fly and build their own nests.

Write **T** if the sentence is true and **F** if it is false.

_____ 1. Every month birds must build a nest for their young.
_____ 2. Birds gather sticks, grass, and feathers to build their nests.
_____ 3. The nests are usually rough.
_____ 4. Baby birds depend on their mother for food.
_____ 5. The mother bird is very busy.
_____ 6. Baby birds usually do not have feathers when they are born.
_____ 7. Baby birds help their mother to build the nest.

Answer the following questions.

8. What color are baby birds when they are born? _____

_____

9. What does a mother bird do if her baby bird falls out of the nest?

_____

_____

10. How does the mother bird build a good nest? _____

_____

11. What does the mother bird do if some of the sticks and grass fall

out of the nest? _____

_____

12. What part of their bodies must young birds learn to use before they

can fly? _____

_____

Follow-up

G. Dictation: Write the sentences that your teacher reads aloud.

1. _____

2. _____

3. _____

4. _____

5. _____

H. Answer the following questions.

1. What things are pink?
2. What has wings?
3. Do you know the names of any stars? Which ones?
4. Which animals have shells?
5. Name some things with rough surfaces.
6. What can you do if you spill something on your clothes?
7. What happens when a boat spills oil?
8. What jobs require considerable creativity?
9. In what occupations do people perform rescue operations?
10. Which events have gatherings of people?
11. When do you need to replace a tire? Your shoes? A carpet?
12. What wild animals are found in your country?

UNIT
20

Religion

Word Form Chart

NOUN	VERB	ADJECTIVE	ADVERB
amazement	amaze	amazing	amazingly
		amazed	
angel		angelic	angelically
blessing	bless	blessed	
		close	close
decoration	decorate	decorated	
decorator		decorating	
funeral		funeral	
grief	grieve	grieving	
		grievous	grievously
mortal		mortal	mortally
mortality			
immortality		immortal	
Lord			
preacher	preach		
priest		priestly	
priestess			
ritual	ritualize	ritualistic	ritualistically
robe		robed	
	disrobe		
		sacred	
spirit		spiritual	spiritually
supremacy		supreme	supremely
worshiper	worship	worshiped	
worship			

Definitions and Examples

1. **blessing** (a) [the act of making something holy]

    The people celebrated the **blessing** of the new church.

    (b) [a wish for success; approval]

    Some people ask for their parents' **blessing** when they get married.

    (c) [a thing that brings happiness]

    Children are often considered a **blessing** to a family.

2. **amaze** [to fill with surprise and wonder]

    Her teachers were **amazed** to see how much she had learned in just
    one year.
    Jack shows **amazing** wisdom for someone so young.

3. **angel** (a) [in some religions, a heavenly being who is a messenger
    of God]

    In religious art, **angels** are often painted with wings.

    (b) [a person who is especially good or kind]

    You are an **angel** for helping me, Martha.

4. **ritual** [the form for a ceremony]

    The medicine man performed an ancient **ritual**.
    Have you seen the **ritual** connected with the lighting of candles?

5. **close** (to) (a) [near in time or space]

    In math class I usually sit **close to** the door.

    (b) [near in a family or relationship]

    I have always felt **close to** my older sister.

6. **decorate** [to make a thing look more attractive by adding something
    nice to it]

    The children usually **decorate** the house for the holidays.
    They use **decorations** made of colored paper.

7. **grief** [a sad feeling about a loss]

    Grief is a common feeling at the death of a relative.
    War causes destruction and **grief**.

8. **Lord** [another word for God in some religions]

    Every day I pray to the **Lord**.

9. **preach** [to talk on a religious subject]

    A holy man can **preach** about God's laws.
    The **preacher** is a well-respected man in this town.

10. **funeral** [the ceremony held for a dead person]

    The president's **funeral** was attended by thousands of people.
    The **funeral** of a family member is often very sad.

11. **priest** [the name for a holy man in some religions; the person who has authority to perform religious ceremonies]

    When my brother became a **priest**, my family was very proud.
    The man who performed our wedding ceremony was a **priest** from a local church.

12. **robe** [a loose, long piece of clothing, sometimes used to show someone's position or rank]

    A priest often wears a long black **robe**.
    My new bath**robe** is made of cotton.

13. **sacred** [holy; religious]

    Sacred music is part of the holidays in some religions.
    The **sacred** books are kept in a safe place.

14. **mortal** [certain to die; capable of causing death]

    All people are **mortal**.
    Young people sometimes act as if they were **immortal**.
    The infant **mortality** rate is falling every year.

15. **spirit** (a) [the force that gives life to the body]

    My grandfather has the **spirit** of a much younger man.

    (b) [in many religions, the immortal part of a living thing]

    Many religions teach that body and **spirit** are separated at the time of death.

16. **spiritual** [having to do with sacred or religious things; relating to the spirit, not the body]

    A religious ceremony is a **spiritual** experience.

17. **supreme** [highest in rank, power, authority]

    A prayer is addressed to a **supreme** being.
    The president is the **supreme** commander of the military.

18. **worship** (a) [to honor, respect, or love]

Martin always **worshipped** his older brothers.

(b) [to take part in a religious ceremony]

Every Sunday we **worship** in a large, beautiful church.

Introductory Exercises

A. Match each word with its definition.

_____ 1. highest in rank

_____ 2. a messenger of God

_____ 3. to fill with wonder

_____ 4. to honor or respect very much

_____ 5. a wish for success

_____ 6. near in time

_____ 7. a sad feeling

_____ 8. a man who performs religious ceremonies

_____ 9. certain to die

_____ 10. a loose piece of clothing

a. amaze
b. angel
c. blessing
d. close to
e. funeral
f. grief
g. mortal
h. preach
i. priest
j. robe
k. supreme
l. worship

B. Answer each question with a word from the word form chart in this ·unit.

1. Who gives talks about religious subjects?
2. What do some people wear to show their rank?
3. What is a thing that brings happiness?
4. What do some people do to their homes for a holiday?
5. What is the ceremony for a dead person called?
6. What is another word for "God" in some religions?
7. What kind of music is played in a church?
8. Who performs weddings and funerals in a church?
9. What can we call a person who is very good and kind?
10. What is the opposite of "far from"?

Study Exercises

C. Write **T** if the sentence is true and **F** if it is false.

_____ 1. Good health is a blessing.

_____ 2. It is appropriate to feel grief at a funeral.

_____ 3. Some people's bodies are immortal.

_____ 4. A priest can perform rituals.

_____ 5. A robe is long.

_____ 6. Brothers and sisters often feel close to each other.

_____ 7. Angels perform selfish acts.

_____ 8. A magician can do some amazing tricks.

_____ 9. Having breakfast is a ceremony.

_____ 10. A baseball game is a spiritual event.

D. In the blanks, write the appropriate word(s) from the word form chart in this unit.

1. They said they would not get married without their parents'

_____ .

2. If I go into the jungle alone, I might be in _____ danger.

3. The streets were _____ with flowers for the annual parade.

4. _____ books are part of many religions.

5. For such an important event, the queen wore a _____ of gold material.

6. Followers of some religions _____ many gods.

7. I read a(n) _____ story about moon rockets.

8. When my grandfather died, I cried at his _____ .

9. The _____ told stories about miracles and mysteries.

10. When I pray I thank the _____ for my blessings.

E. Circle the word or phrase which is different in meaning.

1. surprised   amazed   assigned

2. close to   near   accustomed to

3. grief   sadness   talent

4. Lord   Mr.   God

5. hell   ritual   ceremony

6. holy   enormous   sacred

7. worship   profit   honor

8. supreme   highest   amateur

F.   Read the passage and answer the questions that follow.

I am not a religious person, but I have always been amazed at how hard priests work and how busy their days are. They are responsible for the spiritual lives of the people they are close to. They say the blessings at weddings, and
5 they comfort the grieving families at funerals. Worshipers also expect a priest to preach about good and evil and immortality. During the holiday season, it is especially nice to sit in the decorated church, to hear the sacred music, and to see the priest in his beautiful robe. A priest knows that he
10 is not supremely rich or powerful, but he feels blessed just to be a servant of the Lord.

1. What is the writer amazed at? _____

_____

2. What are priests responsible for? _____

_____

3. What do priests do at weddings? _____

_____

4. Who comforts people at funerals? _____

_____

5. What do priests preach about? _____

_____

6. When is the church decorated? _____

_____

7. What does a priest wear? _____

_____

8. Why does a priest feel blessed? _____

_____

Follow-up

G. Dictation: Write the sentences that your teacher reads aloud.

1. _____

2. _____

3. _____

4. _____

5. _____

H. Listen to the definitions. Say the word from the word form chart.

1. to fill with surprise
2. an especially good person
3. a thing that brings happiness
4. near in a family
5. to make a thing look more attractive
6. the ceremony for a dead person
7. person having power over others
8. the form for a ceremony
9. to take part in a religious ceremony
10. the force that gives life to a body

I.
1. Describe the decorations in your house for a holiday.
2. Describe the ritual of a funeral.
3. Do you know an angel? Describe this person's actions.

Sports

Word Form Chart

NOUN	VERB	ADJECTIVE	ADVERB
aspect			
challenge	challenge	challenging	challengingly
challenger		challenged	
cycle	cycle	cyclic	cyclically
cyclist		cyclical	
grab	grab		
league			
muscle		muscular	
obstacle			
point	point	pointed	
position	position	positioned	
postponement	postpone	postponed	
routine		routine	routinely
rub			
rubbing	rub	rubbing	
		rubbed	
temper		tempered	
tire			
volleyball			
wave	wave	wavy	
whole		whole	wholly

Definitions and Examples

1. **league** [an organization of teams or other groups]

   There are twelve teams in our baseball **league**.
   We won all of our **league** games but lost two games against opponents from outside the **league**.
   The **League** of Women Voters is planning a meeting for next Thursday.

2. **grab** (onto) [to take a hold of something suddenly; to get]

   The player **grabbed onto** his teammate so that he would not fall down.
   In pain, the athlete **grabbed** his ankle and screamed.
   The thief **grabbed** the lady's purse and ran down the street.

3. **rub** [to move something forwards and then backwards against another surface]

   When he is nervous, he always **rubs** his hands together.
   My tennis shoes are **rubbing** my feet so much that my toes are beginning to hurt.
   The runner **rubbed** his legs to keep them warm.

4. **routine** (a) [a usual method of procedure; habit]

   The athletes go through an exercise **routine** before every game to help them warm up.
   We follow the same **routine** every morning and afternoon.

   (b) [lacking in interest or originality]

   It is such a **routine** meeting that it is hardly worth our time.

5. **obstacle** [anything that keeps you from reaching an end result]

   Lack of money and organization is frequently an **obstacle** for young teams.
   If you really want something, you will not allow **obstacles** to prevent you from getting it; you will do what you can to work around the **obstacles**.

6. **wave** [to move up and down or from side to side]

   The crowds screamed and **waved** their arms as the players came onto the field.
   The national flag was **waved** about the field.
   The swimmer rode the **wave** of water until it finally crashed onto the beach.

7. **muscle** [the parts of the body that control body movement and that help determine how strong you are]

> After the game, all of the **muscles** in his arms and legs were aching.
> The tennis player could hit the ball hard because his **muscles** were so strong.

8. **temper** [a state of mind or emotions; mood]

> He has a very bad **temper**; he gets angry when the smallest thing goes wrong.
> Everyone in my family is good **tempered**.
> You must always try to control your **temper** in public.
> "To lose your **temper**" means "to get angry."

9. **postpone** [to change the time for a planned event to a later time]

> We **postponed** the game because of the rain.
> The concert was **postponed** until next Friday because the lead singer had a sore throat.
> When the teacher realized that none of the students understood the chapter, she **postponed** the test.

10. **challenging** [requiring complete use of your abilities]

> The game was not too difficult, but it was **challenging** enough to be fun.
> We like playing strong opponents because it is more of a **challenge** for us.

11. **challenge** (a) [to call an opponent to compete]

> To prove that he was faster than his friend, John **challenged** him to a race.

> (b) [to demand an explanation]

> I **challenged** his reasons for doing what he did.

12. **volleyball** [a sport using a large ball which is passed back and forth between two teams of six players each; the ball itself]

> In the last fifteen years, **volleyball** has become extremely popular around the world.
> In **volleyball**, each team can contact the ball a maximum of three times before they have to hit the ball back to the other team.

13. **point** (a) [a number in a score]

> We scored five more **points** than our opponents; the final score was
> 15–10.
> To win a volleyball game you must have fifteen **points**, and you
> must have two more **points** than your opponents.

(b) [to signal with your finger in order to show somebody something]

> The man **pointed** to where our seats were.
> It's impolite to **point** at people.

(c) [the purpose; the reason]

> I do not understand the **point** of writing this 30-page report if no
> one is going to read it.
> There is no **point** in arguing with him; he will never change his
> opinion.
> A: What's the **point** of so much practice?
> B: So that we can beat our strongest opponents.

14. **whole** [entire; complete]

> We were not able to stay for the **whole** game.
> The **whole** team felt terrible that they had lost against such weak
> opponents.
> The children cried the **whole** way home.

15. **aspect** [a part; a characteristic]

> There are many **aspects** of this sport that the fans are unaware of.
>
> A: What **aspects** of this city do you like the most?
> B: The people are friendly, and there's always a lot to do.

16. **cycle** (a) [to ride a bicycle]

> They **cycle** over 100 miles each week.
> The **cyclists** prepared to begin the race.
> **Cycling** in the city can be dangerous.

(b) [a period of time during which a characteristic event or series of
events occurs]

> The seasons run in a **cycle**: spring, winter, summer, fall.
> The life **cycle** can be divided into different parts: birth, childhood,
> adulthood, old age, death.

17. **tire** [a solid or air-filled covering for a wheel]

> The cyclist hit a rock and got a flat **tire**.
> Good **tires** will help keep a car safely on the road even in the worst
> of weather conditions.

18. **position** (a) [a player's area of responsibility; a place or location]

>   A: What **position** does he play?
>   B: He usually plays center field.

>   He is so talented that he can play in any **position** for our team.

(b) [the way in which something is placed]

>   My mother does not like it when I sit in this **position**; she says it is very bad for my back.

(c) [to place something in a certain way]

>   We **positioned** everyone close together so that everyone would fit into the photograph.

(d) [a point of view; opinion]

>   From our **position**, there was no problem; we could not understand why everyone was so angry.

>   A: What **position** are you taking on this issue?
>   B: I think that students who get low grades should not be allowed to compete in school sports until their grades improve.

Introductory Exercises

A. Match each word with its definition.

_____ **1.** a movement of the hand

_____ **2.** an organization

_____ **3.** anything that keeps you from reaching a result easily

_____ **4.** to move until a later time

_____ **5.** requiring all your abilities

_____ **6.** part of the body

_____ **7.** a state of mind or emotions

_____ **8.** to take quickly

_____ **9.** the purpose of something

_____ **10.** complete or entire

a. aspect
b. challenging
c. grab
d. league
e. muscle
f. obstacle
g. point
h. postpone
i. rub
j. temper
k. wave
l. whole

B. Answer **TRUE** or **FALSE**.

1. When you postpone an event, you have it earlier.
2. Climbing a mountain can be a great challenge.
3. A car tire is made of metal.

4. A league is the same as a team.
5. Any activities that you do the same way over a period of time can be called a routine.
6. Your position on a subject is your opinion on it.
7. You should not rub a cut in your skin.
8. Children with bad tempers frequently kick and bite.
9. Muscles help you control the movement of body parts.
10. One aspect of a language is its word order.

Study Exercises

C. In the blanks, write the appropriate word(s) from the word form chart in this unit.

1. She cried the _____ way home.

2. _____ exercises make you use your whole ability.

3. It is impolite to _____ things away from other people.

4. He could not sleep because he was unable to get into a comfortable _____ .

5. Because the weather was bad, the teams _____ the game.

6. This class is boring because we always follow the same

   _____ .

7. When he saw me, he _____ his hand.

8. Lack of money is the main _____ in our way.

9. It is difficult to live with someone who has a bad

   _____ and gets angry a lot.

10. The cat _____ its head and back against the chair.

11. That disease follows an obvious _____ ; first you get a headache, then a cough, then a fever.

D. From the following definitions and clues determine which words are in the Word Challenge Box. Then mark each word in the box. The first two have been done for you.

1. complete   _____whole_____

2. a score   _____point_____

3. sport with a large ball   _____

4. sports team organization   _____

5. your opinion   _____

6. something in your way   _____

7. some people have a calm one; some people have an angry one   _____

8. having large muscles   _____

9. the same way every time   _____

10. to get a hold of   _____

11. riding a bicycle   _____

12. requiring you to work hard   _____

13. a particular part of something   _____

14. the black part around a wheel   _____

15. to make a new and later time   _____

16. a hand movement   _____

17. to move something back and forth against something else   _____

WORD CHALLENGE BOX

```
T C H A L L E N G I N G P O I N T L
E Q F D P Q R C T Y H B J I O M K E
M C O C Y C L I N G B C Y X J A F D
P E G D R Q R S R O U T I N E S D N
E B T G R A B S T U T U V W H P G M
R O P H L M I K J J T I K P V E C C
W O R D C H A L L E N G E O W C O M
N B F N V U R T J T P I H S Q P X U
M S G L H K P R Q I U O L T R W B S
O T U V E X O W S R N V M P G H Y C
Z A Y W N I S D C E L M N O F O E U
A C T X D M I E N E R G Y N T L S L
P L L C P O T A E N W A V E Z E U A
L E A G U E I W X F G H X A V W D R
A Z B Q B K O J K J I Y Z R U B A C
W Z R A S Y N V O L L E Y B A L L B
```

E.   Read the passage and answer the questions that follow.

> Thousands of college students around the United States participate in intercollegiate athletics. Many people believe that student-athletes spend too much time on their sports and not enough on their classes, but the benefits that
> 5 students gain from athletics are far greater than most people realize.
>
> The most obvious benefits are the physical changes. The whole body grows stronger. Not only does an athlete become more muscular, but the capacity of his heart and lungs
> 10 increases as well. Because his body is stronger, an athlete gets tired less often, needs to eat less food, and generally has more energy than a nonathlete.
>
> Participation in athletics also provides emotional and social benefits for students. Sports teach an athlete to control
> 15 his temper and to get along with others. Each player must follow certain rules and cooperate with the other players on his team if he expects to win. Sports also teach an athlete to accept challenges and face obstacles with determination. Strong opponents help an athlete play to the best of his
> 20 abilities, make decisions quickly, and gain confidence. In addition, participation in sports teaches a student to organize his time wisely and to follow a routine that will help him meet his responsibilities on time.
>
> In short, participation in athletics is extremely beneficial
> 25 for college students physically and emotionally and socially as well. The lessons that an athlete learns from sports will remain with him his whole life.

1. What complaint do some people have about college athletes? _____

_____

2. What are the three types of benefits that participation in sports

provides? _____

_____

3. What are the physical benefits? _____

_____

4. What happens when the body is stronger? _____

_____

5. What emotional benefits does participation in sports provide? _____

_____

6. What personal and social skills can an athlete use in the working

world? _____

_____

Follow-up

F.   Dictation: Write the sentences that your teacher reads aloud.

1. _____

2. _____

3. _____

4. _____

5. _____

G.   Complete the following sentences with a word from the word form chart in this unit.

1. The change from spring to summer, to fall, to winter and back to spring is an example of a(n) _____ .

2. If you don't have time right now to do something you can _____ it.

3. The opposite of part is _____ .

4. When you stop being calm, you may lose your _____ .

5. Teaching children is the program's whole _____ .

6. Someone who rides a bike is a(n) _____ .

7. Various characteristics of something are its _____ .

8. How something is arranged or placed is its _____ .

9. Race cars use special _____ .

10. People frequently indicate where something is by _____ .

11. Something that is a little difficult creates a(n) _____ .

12. Something that is so difficult that you can't continue creates

   a(n) _____ .

H.   Answer the following questions.

   1. What kind of sports leagues are there in your hometown?
   2. What is your morning routine?
   3. What is the greatest obstacle you have faced in your life?
   4. How do you deal with challenging situations?
   5. What can make you lose your temper?
   6. What do you do when your life becomes too routine?
   7. What aspects of sports do you like?
   8. What aspects of the reading in Exercise E do you agree with?
      Disagree with?
   9. What is your position on professional sports? The money involved?
      The danger to the athletes?
   10. Do you follow a regular exercise routine which develops particular
       muscles? Which ones?

Banking

Word Form Chart

NOUN	VERB	ADJECTIVE	ADVERB
accumulation	accumulate	accumulated accumulating	
acquisition	acquire	acquired	
asset			
check	check		
currency			
deadline			
deduction	deduct	deductible	
	deduce	deductive	deductively
	figure out		
	find out (found out, found out)		
fortune			
gamble	gamble	gambled gambling	
gambler			
guarantee	guarantee	guaranteed	
investment	invest	invested	
investor			
loan	loan		
matter	matter		
rudeness		rude	rudely
teller			
term(s)			
treasure	treasure	treasured	
treasury			
treasurer			
upset	upset (upset, upset)	upset	

Definitions and Examples

1. **currency** [money]

    The exchange rates for foreign **currency** change daily.
    Stores in some border towns accept the **currency** of two different countries.

2. **loan** [something that is borrowed, especially money borrowed at interest]

    A **loan** must always be repaid.
    "To **loan**" is the same as "to lend."

    A: Are you going to buy a new car?
    B: No. The bank didn't give me a **loan**, so I can't afford it.

3. **teller** [a clerk in a bank]

    Tellers are the bank employees who receive deposits from customers and cash customers' checks.

    A: Did your sister find a job?
    B: Yes. She's a **teller** at First National Bank. Her salary is low, but she likes the contact with people.

4. **rude** [not polite]

    In the United States, it is **rude** not to look at someone who is talking to you.

    A: Which bank do you go to?
    B: First National. I used to go to City Bank, but the tellers were so **rude** that I changed.

5. **fortune** [a lot of money and possessions]

    The Rockefeller family made its **fortune** in the oil business.

    A: Where did Charles get his money?
    B: Well, he's worked hard, but he also inherited his rich uncle's **fortune**.

6. **gamble** [to take a chance, often in a dangerous situation; to bet money on a game or event]

    Las Vegas is the **gambling** capital of the United States.

    A: Do you ever **gamble** on sporting events?
    B: No. Once I bet on a basketball game, but I lost a fortune and decided never to **gamble** again.

7. **acquire** [to get possession of; to obtain or develop an ability]

> An easy way to **acquire** a language is to live in the country where it is spoken.
> The art museum is currently showing its recent **acquisitions** from China.

8. **asset** [a useful or valuable quality or possession; an advantage]

> The company's **assets** include everything it owns and the money it has in the bank.
> Banks like to loan money to people who have many **assets**.
> Your past experience in this kind of work will be a great **asset** when you apply for another job.

9. **invest** [to spend or use time, money, or effort because you expect a future profit]

> Land is usually considered to be a safe **investment**.
> **Investment** consultants tell people how to use their money to make the biggest profit.
>
> A: Have you finished that project already?
> B: Almost. I don't want to **invest** much time in it because it's not very important.

10. **figure out** {informal} (a) {separable} [to solve, often by mathematical calculation]

> The new teller could not **figure out** the account balance until the boss explained it to her.
>
> A: What's wrong?
> B: I can't **figure out** the answer without a powerful computer, and I don't have one.

{b} {separable} [to understand after a lot of effort]

> I do not understand why the new teacher quit. None of the other students can **figure** it **out** either.

11. **deduct** [to subtract]

> The United States government **deducts** money for taxes from every worker's paycheck.
> The bank **deducted** $7 from my account when I wrote a check without enough money. The **deduction** was to pay for the bank's extra work.

12. **find out** (a) {separable} [to learn by studying or watching]

> You can **find out** about a bank's reputation by talking to its customers.

(b) {separable} [to acquire new information by chance]

> Today is the last day to get a loan at low interest rates. Fortunately, I **found out** before it was too late.

> A: How did Peter **find out** about his surprise birthday party?
> B: He **found** it **out** from Carol. She didn't know it was a surprise.

13. **accumulate** [to increase in amount gradually; to collect gradually]

> My uncle **accumulated** a fortune by investing wisely and spending little.
> If a house is not cleaned regularly, dust **accumulates** everywhere.

14. **guarantee** [a promise that a person or company is responsible for the good quality of something]

> My new refrigerator is **guaranteed** for five years. If it breaks during that time, the manufacturer will repair or replace it.

> A: Why does the bank want my parents' signature on my loan application?
> B: The bank wants a **guarantee** of repayment. If you don't pay, your parents will have to.

15. **check** (a) [to examine or inspect, often in order to find out if something is correct]

> Teachers **check** students' papers to see if students have understood the material.

> A: I'm not sure how much money I have in my account.
> B: Ask the teller to **check** your balance.

(b) [this mark: √]

> The teacher marked wrong answers with a **check**.
> The bank inspector put a **check** next to each item on the list that he had examined.

(c) [3-13: A form of payment used instead of cash]

> Not all stores will accept checks.

16. **deduce** [to figure out by calculation from facts]

> From the clues, Mr. Holmes **deduced** who the criminal was.
> I made a wrong **deduction** from his statements, so I became confused.

17. **upset** (a) [unhappy or angry]

> The rude teller **upset** the customer.
> People get **upset** when they hear bad news.
> Mrs. Schafer was **upset** when she found out about her husband's gambling.

   (b) [to turn something out of its usual position]

> The child **upset** the small boat when he stood up in it.

> A: Why does this loan report have a brown spot on it?
> B: I accidentally **upset** my coffee cup on it.

18. **treasure** [something precious, of great value]

> **Treasure**-hunters went to California in 1849 to find gold.
> My grandmother **treasures** her photographs of her grandchildren.

19. **matter** (a) [an issue to be considered; something important]

> Investing money is a serious **matter**. People should think wisely about it and consult experts if possible.
> "It doesn't **matter**" means "It isn't important."

   (b) [problem; difficulty]

> A: What's the **matter**?
> B: Oh, nothing.
> A: There must be something wrong. You seem upset.

   (c) [material; something that has weight and fills space]

> Physicists study the laws which govern **matter**.

20. **deadline** [the date or time by which something must be finished]

> The **deadline** for giving the bank this loan application is 5 P.M. Friday. The bank will not accept it after that time.

> Student: Could you please extend the **deadline** for this paper?
> Teacher: No. I'm sorry. You must finish it by next Tuesday.

21. **term** [a period of time]

> The normal **term** for a loan for a house is thirty years.
> A United States president's **term** in office is four years.
> Most universities in the United States begin their programs in the fall **term**.

22. **terms** {usually plural} [rules of agreement; conditions]

> The **terms** of this loan are three years at seven percent interest.

> A: What were the **terms** of the peace agreement?
> B: I don't know. The president announced that both sides had compromised, but the details aren't public yet.

Introductory Exercises

A. Match each word with its definition.

____	1. not polite	**a.** accumulate
____	2. a period of time	**b.** acquire
____	3. to increase gradually	**c.** assets
____	4. to spend money in expectation of profit	**d.** check
____	5. to get possession of	**e.** currency
____	6. a lot of wealth	**f.** deadline
____	7. to subtract	**g.** deduct
____	8. to solve	**h.** figure out
____	9. a promise to be responsible	**i.** find out
____	10. an issue to be considered	**j.** fortune
____	11. to examine or inspect	**k.** guarantee
____	12. unhappy or angry	**l.** invest
____	13. something of great value	**m.** loan
____	14. a clerk in a bank	**n.** matter
____	15. money	**o.** rude
____	16. money and possessions	**p.** teller
		q. term
		r. treasure
		s. upset

B. Answer each question with a word from the word form chart in this unit.

1. What is a person who bets on games and races?
2. What do you need from the bank to buy something expensive?
3. Describe a person who is impolite.
4. How do you feel if someone is rude to you?
5. When is the time that something is due?
6. What are the details of an agreement?
7. What kind of agreement says who is responsible for fixing a product?
8. What is something that you can figure out from a general rule?
9. If you need information that you do not have, what should you do?
10. What can you do with your money to make a profit?
11. What do you do with a difficult problem?
12. What is a period of time?

Study Exercises

C. Write **T** if the sentence is true and **F** if it is false.

_____ 1. A teller is someone who talks a lot.

_____ 2. You may be upset if someone is rude to you.

_____ 3. Gambling is a good way to have a guaranteed income.

_____ 4. If you invest wisely, you may accumulate a fortune.

_____ 5. When you add two numbers, you deduct one from the other.

_____ 6. Eliminating pollution is a short-term problem.

_____ 7. Things usually accumulate suddenly.

_____ 8. A family may need a loan to acquire a house.

_____ 9. Rudeness is an asset for any employee.

_____ 10. If the deadline for a payment is tomorrow, you should pay today or tomorrow.

_____ 11. The treasurer of an organization controls the money.

D. Circle the word which is different in meaning.

1. deduct   accumulate   acquire
2. treasure   fortune   loan
3. upset   asset   angry
4. guarantee   promise   gamble
5. learn   matter   find out
6. term   figure out   calculate
7. check   investigate   rude
8. invest   deadline   spend
9. subtract   deduct   deduce

E. Read the news items and answer the questions that follow.

News Item:
   Officials at the National Treasury today announced new restrictions on foreign investment in this country. Beginning next year, foreign investors will be permitted to acquire only
5 40% of any company here. Investors must present a detailed list of their assets to the Treasury Office showing their bank balances, buildings and equipment that they own, and other

information. They must also guarantee that 70% of their employees will be natives of this country.

10   Local business people have protested that investment is a private matter and should not be controlled by the government.

1. How much of a company will foreign investors be able to

buy? _____

_____

2. What examples of assets are given in this article? _____

_____

3. What must the foreign investor promise? _____

_____

4. What do local business people think about this decision? _____

_____

News Item:
"Taxes will increase next year." That announcement came from the leaders of both political parties today. "We have been fortunate for the last few years," they said, "but

5   we can no longer guarantee that taxes will remain stable."
Michael Huffman, an expert on personal money matters, advises, "People should not get upset about this announcement until they have more information. It will still be possible for each taxpayer to make a variety of deductions

10   from the total tax amount. It is impossible to figure out the exact increase in anyone's taxes at this time."

Write **T** if the sentence is true and **F** if it is false.

_____ **5.** Leaders promise that taxes will remain stable.

_____ **6.** In the last few years, taxpayers have been lucky.

_____ **7.** Michael Huffman knows a lot about banking and money.

_____ **8.** Mr. Huffman thinks people should worry about this increase.

_____ **9.** With the new taxes, people will not be able to subtract anything from the amount they owe.

_____ **10.** People cannot calculate their new taxes accurately now.

Follow-up

F. Dictation: Write the sentences that your teacher reads aloud.

1. _____

2. _____

3. _____

4. _____

5. _____

G. For each blank, give a word from the word form chart in this unit.

1. News reporting is a stressful job because of the need to be on time. Reporters must meet strict _____ .

2. The bank will not give you a loan unless you have _____ .

3. Some people do not like to throw anything away. They just _____ more and more things.

4. You can _____ about making cheese by visiting a dairy.

5. Charles became rich when he found a buried _____ in a cave during his vacation.

6. Smoking is _____ with your health.

7. During sales something is _____ from the original prices.

8. My new watch is _____ against all problems for one year.

H. Answer the following questions.

1. What makes you upset?
2. Do you usually meet deadlines? What kind of deadline is hard for you to meet?
3. Have you ever invested money in a long-term project? Explain.
4. What kinds of products come with a guarantee?
5. What is the main unit of currency in your country?
6. Which of your possessions do you treasure?

I. Finish the story. Tell what will happen.

A young man applies for a loan to invest in some land.

Education (B)

Word Form Chart

NOUN	VERB	ADJECTIVE	ADVERB	PREPOSITION
abstraction		abstract	abstractly	
assumption	assume	assumed		
				beyond
capability		capable (of)	capably	
chairman	chair			
		chief	chiefly	
civilization	civilize	civilized		
		civilizing		
code				
concept	conceptualize	conceptual	conceptually	
conception				
conference	confer	conferring		
essay				
greeting	greet			
mark	mark	marked		
master	master	masterful	masterfully	
pace	pace			
pacing				
philosophy	philosophize	philosophical	philosophically	
philosopher				
prediction	predict	predictable	predictably	
qualification	qualify	qualified		
		qualifying		
rejection	reject	rejected		
theory	theorize	theoretical	theoretically	

Definitions and Examples

1. **theory** [a system of assumptions that predicts or explains something]

   Some students do well in the practical work but do not do well in **theory**.

   Your side is fine in **theory**, but it will not work in practice.

   Our **theoretical** assumptions had to be revised as a result of the latest research.

2. **abstract** [not concrete; theoretical]

   It is hard to define **abstract** ideas like "democracy" and "truth."

   A: How did you like the lecture?

   B: I couldn't follow it. It was too **abstract**.

3. **assume** [to take something as true]

   We **assume** that our students have a basic knowledge of mathematics.

   The examination policy is based on the **assumption** that students are basically honest.

4. **beyond** [on the far side of; past something]

   Visitors are not allowed **beyond** this point.

   A: I could never understand calculus. It's **beyond** me.

   B: Well, you should study something that will take you **beyond** what you already know.

5. **mark** (a) [to assign a grade for school work]

   She always got high **marks** in geology.

   The professor **marked** the papers very strictly. There were a lot of low **marks** in the class.

   (b) [4-6: a spot]

   The white paint left a **mark** on her dress.

6. **capable** (of) [having the ability to do something]

   She is **capable of** doing much better work.

   A: What do you think of your chemistry instructor?

   B: Oh, she's **capable** enough, but she's so boring.

7. **chairman** [the head of a committee or a meeting or a university department]

>   The **chairman** of the department will make the final decision on admissions.

>   A: Who were you talking to just now?
>   B: She's the **chairman** of our department.

>   The words "chair" and "chairperson" are sometimes used instead of **chairman**.
>   The word "chairwoman" is often used when the chairperson is a woman.

8. **greet** [to say something friendly to the people you meet]

>   The professor **greeted** the class with a pleasant "Good morning!"
>   The members of the committee exchanged **greetings** before they sat down to work.

9. **chief** [principal; most important]

>   Our **chief** aim is to provide undergraduates with a good education.
>   The **chief** disadvantage of that school is its high tuition.

10. **essay** [a short piece of writing on a single subject]

>   As part of the application, students are asked to write an **essay** about their educational objectives.

>   A: What kind of test was it?
>   B: All **essay** questions.

11. **civilization** [a high stage of social development]

>   Students should know something about the major **civilizations** of the world.
>   A great **civilization** existed here many thousands of years ago.

12. **code** (a) [a collection of rules for behavior]

>   The school has a strict **code** for students.
>   It is the responsibility of the students to follow the honor **code**.

>>   (b) [3-5: letters, numbers, or symbols that have a special meaning]

>>   The area **code** is part of your telephone number.

13. **conference** [a meeting where opinions are exchanged]

>   The chairman had individual **conferences** with the staff.
>   The professor attended a national **conference** on electrical engineering.

14. **qualified** [capable; meeting the requirements of something]

All our students are fully **qualified** to teach in the public schools.
He is not as well **qualified** for the job as the former chairman.
If you are the best **qualified** person, you should get the job.

15. **master** [to become very skilled at something]

After many years of trying, Mary finally **mastered** calculus.
Students are expected to acquire **mastery** of the basic skills of good
    writing.

16. **philosophy** [the investigation of knowledge; a set of beliefs]

We had to read about the Greek **philosophers**.
Her **philosophy** of education is very different from mine.

17. **concept** [an idea or a thought]

Students are supposed to know the basic **concepts** of their field.
The textbook does not explain the **concepts** very well.

18. **conception** [a mental picture of some abstract idea]

My **conception** of democracy differs from yours.
I am having a problem **conceptualizing** it.
Conceptually, it is simple.

A: Where is he, anyway?
B: He's always late. He has no **conception** of time.

19. **predict** [to tell what will happen]

We **predict** that about twenty percent of the students will fail to
    graduate.
The weather around here is **unpredictable**.

20. **reject** [to refuse to accept or consider something]

The university **rejected** her application.
The professor **rejected** the student's request to reschedule the exam.

21. **pace** [the speed at which something or someone goes]

Some teachers go at a fast **pace**.
Some of the students did not like the **pace** of the class; it was too
    slow.

A: I like this calculus class.
B: It's too fast-**paced** for me.

Introductory Exercises

A. Match each word with its definition.

_____ 1. having ability

_____ 2. a high level of social development

_____ 3. a meeting

_____ 4. an idea or thought

_____ 5. to assign a grade

_____ 6. a short piece of writing

_____ 7. meeting the requirements of something

_____ 8. to tell what will happen

_____ 9. to refuse to accept

_____ 10. the speed at which something goes

_____ 11. a set of beliefs

_____ 12. a collection of rules for behavior

_____ 13. principal; most important

_____ 14. not concrete

_____ 15. to take something as true

a. abstract
b. assume
c. beyond
d. capable of
e. chairman
f. chief
g. civilization
h. code
i. concept
j. conference
k. essay
l. greet
m. mark
n. master
o. pace
p. philosophy
q. predict
r. qualified
s. reject
t. theory

B. Answer the questions with a word from the word form chart in this unit.

1. What might a teacher ask you to write?
2. What do you do when you see someone you know?
3. How would you describe a person who is capable of doing a job?
4. What would you do if someone offered you a job that paid too little?
5. How would you describe a class that goes very fast?
6. Where might you hear professors talk about their research?
7. What do you call a set of ideas that allows you to explain something?
8. What do you call the head of a department in a university?
9. Who was Aristotle?
10. What word describes concepts like "liberty" or "justice?"

Study Exercises

C. In the blanks, write the appropriate word(s) from the word form chart in this unit.

1. She got high _____ on the last exam.
2. The _____ of the class was too fast.
3. To _____ the subject of chemistry, you have to study for a long time.
4. Her practical experience is fine, but she lacks a good _____ background.
5. Your students are _____ of getting better grades.
6. Physics is _____ me. I'll never learn it.
7. I _____ he was the professor. He didn't say he was one.
8. The _____ difficulty I had was with English. My other subjects were easy.
9. The university _____ my application. They said I sent it too late.
10. The department chairman went to a _____ to read a research paper.
11. Applicants are required to write an _____ about their educational interests.
12. The code of honor is based on the _____ that students will be honest.
13. You should know something about the major _____ of the world.

D. Write **T** if the sentence is true and **F** if it is false.

____ 1. "Water" and "bread" refer to abstract concepts.
____ 2. People usually greet each other by saying "Good-bye."
____ 3. A fast-paced lecture is more difficult to understand than a slower one.
____ 4. If the university rejects your application, you should plan to go there next year.
____ 5. A good theory allows you to predict what will happen.
____ 6. A theory may be shown to rest on false assumptions.
____ 7. The most capable person will probably not do the job well.
____ 8. Philosophy is not very abstract.

_____ **9.** If chemistry is beyond you, you probably get very high marks on chemistry exams.

_____ **10.** It usually takes a long time to acquire mastery of an academic field.

E. Circle the word which is different in meaning.

1. code   law   mark
2. greeting   essay   writing
3. conference   concept   idea
4. capable   chief   qualified
5. confer   comment   meet
6. mark   grade   pace
7. theoretical   chief   important
8. master   chair   learn
9. assume   predict   forecast
10. pace   speed   win

F. Read the passage and answer the questions that follow.

The following is a letter from a college president to possible new students.

Dear High School Seniors:

Thank you for expressing an interest in Brackster College. We are proud of the high quality of the education we
5 offer, and we are confident that our graduates leave the college well equipped to succeed in the careers they choose to enter.
    Let me take a moment to state our educational philosophy. Our chief aim is academic excellence. At the
10 same time, we have developed a program that emphasizes independent thinking, intellectual honesty, and high moral standards. The qualities we look for in applicants are academic ability, honesty, and moral character. While Brackster encourages freedom of ideas, students follow a
15 strict code of honor which regulates behavior both in and out of the classroom.
    Our academic demands are great. Students are expected to come here with a good foundation in science, math, history, and English. The ability to express yourself clearly is
20 crucial. That is one of the reasons why we ask you to include

in your application an essay describing your educational background and interests.

If you come to Brackster, you will become more familiar with the major civilizations of the world, philosophical
25 systems, and scientific concepts that have helped to form the twentieth century. All students are required to take courses in a variety of areas. Our purpose is to prepare you in a wide range of subjects with an emphasis on mastering basic concepts and skills that will lead you to develop your
30 problem-solving ability and critical analysis.

Brackster College does not prepare students for specific careers. We do not train engineers, computer scientists, teachers, managers, or business people. Our conception of higher education is that it should prepare young people to
35 think critically and make intelligent decisions. It is our belief that such students are able to succeed in a variety of careers and are capable of changing careers with little difficulty.

In addition to a life of lectures, tests, laboratories, and term papers, we make an effort at Brackster to develop a
40 close working relationship between students and professors. Regular individual conferences are encouraged. Classes are small, and the campus is small enough to allow frequent interaction between students and professors.

Sports and other outside activities are fully supported by
45 the college. Nearly all our students take part in one or more activities. The college is located in the mountains, and winter sports are especially popular here.

In short, we feel that Brackster College presents a rare educational opportunity to students of a wide variety of
50 interests and backgrounds. If, after reading our informational materials, you would like to apply, please fill out the forms and return them, with accompanying documents, to the Office of the Registrar.

Sincerely,

P. K. Rutledge.

Philip K. Rutledge
President
Brackster College

Questions:

1. Who is the president of the college writing to? Why is he

writing? _____

_____

2. What kind of students go to Brackster College? _____

_____

3. What are the qualities the president looks for in new

students? _____

_____

4. What are the students being prepared to do? _____

_____

5. Why do you think applicants need to write an essay? _____

_____

6. What kind of career would this college train you for? _____

_____

7. What are the advantages of this kind of education? _____

_____

8. What are the disadvantages? _____

_____

9. What can you say about the geography and weather of the area in

which the college is located? _____

_____

Follow-up

G. Dictation: Write the sentences that your teacher reads aloud.

1. _____

2. _____

3. _____

4. _____

5. _____

H. Listen to the definition. Say the word from the word form chart in this unit that matches the definition.

1. an idea or thought
2. on the far side of; past something
3. a system of assumptions that predicts or explains something
4. the investigation of knowledge; a set of beliefs
5. a short piece of writing
6. capable; meeting the requirements of something
7. head of a committee or university department
8. to take something as true
9. a collection of rules for behavior
10. to say something friendly to the people you meet

I. Answer the following questions.

1. Did your college or university prepare you for a career?
2. Do you believe that a university should offer career training?
3. Would you like to go to a college like Brackster College? Why?
4. Do the colleges and universities in your country usually have large numbers of students?
5. Would you prefer a small college? Why?
6. Do students in your country have "honor codes" that regulate behavior?
7. Do professors in your country have close working or social relationships with students?
8. Do colleges and universities in your country differ widely in their educational philosophies?
9. Are sports and outside activities a part of higher education in your country?
10. Do colleges in your country take responsibility for developing the moral character of students?

Transportation (B)

Word Form Chart

NOUN	VERB	ADJECTIVE	PREPOSITION
			along
brake	brake	braking	
dent	dent	dented	
			despite
development	develop	developed	
		developing	
drag	drag	dragging	
freight			
highway			
nod	nod	nodding	
pedal	pedal		
platform			
press	press	pressed	
pressure			
roll	roll	rolled	
		rolling	
scratch	scratch	scratched	
tip	tip		
		steep	
		urban	

Definitions and Examples

1. **dent** [a small mark or hole in something, usually caused by hitting]

   > My car has a **dent** in it; someone must have hit it in the parking lot while I was at the store.
   > The metal table in our kitchen is in good condition generally, but it has a few **dents** on the top.
   > The child **dented** his bicycle when he hit the fence.

2. **along** (a) [following the path]

   > The two children walked **along** the side of the road on their way home.
   > On our vacation we spent hours walking **along** the beach.

   (b) [with, or as a companion]

   > I wanted to go swimming at my friend's pool, but I had forgotten to bring my bathing suit **along**.

   > A: I'm having a party this Saturday. I'd like you to come, and please bring your boyfriend **along**.
   > B: Thank you. I'm sure he'd love to come.

3. **brake** [a device for slowing down or stopping a machine or a vehicle]

   > All cars have **brakes** that are operated by foot; every car should also have a hand **brake** for emergency use.
   > You might have an accident if you **brake** too fast.

4. **develop** (a) [to expand something and make it better, more complete, and more complicated; to grow]

   > The government spent a lot of money to **develop** the national highway system.
   > You can **develop** your vocabulary by reading a lot.
   > In a housing **development**, a builder constructs a lot of new houses on an empty area of land. **Developments** occur in rapidly growing cities.

   (b) [to turn photographic film into pictures]

   > The store near my house **develops** film in one hour.

   > A: How much does it cost to **develop** film at that store?
   > B: About twenty cents a picture.

5. **nod** [to move your head up and down]

> Americans **nod** their heads to mean "yes;" they shake their heads to mean "no."
> Sometimes people **nod** their heads when they fall asleep while reading or watching TV.
> The old lady did not understand my words, but she understood the **nod** of my head to mean "yes."

6. **despite**

> **Despite** the cold weather, my friend Jeanie always walks two miles to school in the winter.
> I would like to take a vacation in New York City, **despite** the expensive prices there.
> John complained a lot about his French class, but **despite** his complaints, he learned a lot.

7. **drag** [to pull or move slowly or with force]

> The small child **dragged** the chair to the kitchen cabinet so that she could reach a piece of cake.
> The two men tried to **drag** the old car along the street, but the car was too heavy.

8. **freight** [a load carried from one place to another in a vehicle such as a truck or a train]

> Agricultural and manufactured products are the most common kinds of **freight** transported by train.
> Trains in the United States carry more **freight** than passengers today.
> It is usually cheaper to send **freight** by sea than by air.

9. **highway** [a large, important road, usually connecting one city to another]

> A **highway** is usually the fastest road between two cities.
> Some **highways** are paid for by the state and some by the national government.

10. roll (a) [to move something by turning it over and over; to move smoothly on wheels]

> The student was nervous while speaking with the professor, and he kept **rolling** his pencil between his hands.
> My dining room table is very heavy, but it has wheels on the legs so I can **roll** it into another room when I clean the dining room.
> The oranges fell off the truck and **rolled** down the street.

(b) [a kind of small bread made by rolling]

> My family always has sweet **rolls** for breakfast on Sunday.

> A: Do you ever make **rolls**?
> B: No. It takes too long to make them. I buy them from the store near my house.

11. pedal [a part that is pushed by the foot to make something work]

> The **pedals** of a bicycle turn the wheels.
> The children had a race to see who could **pedal** the fastest.
> In a car, the gas **pedal** is on the right, and the brake **pedal** is on the left.

12. platform (a) [a raised surface]

> In a railroad station, the **platform** is where people get off and on the trains.
> We waited for the foreign student at **Platform** #2 (number two) at the bus station.

(b) [a raised floor for performers]

> The school auditorium has a special **platform** for speakers.

13. scratch (a) [to make a small cut with something sharp]

> The man **scratched** the paint of his new car with his key.
> When we went camping last week, I got several deep **scratches** on my legs from the woods.

(b) [to rub your skin with your fingernails]

> The child was **scratching** his arm where an insect had bitten him.

> Mother: Don't **scratch** your arm.
> Child: But it's irritating me.
> Mother: You'll only make it worse if you continue to **scratch** it.

14. press (a) [to push on something or to put force on something]

> In an elevator, **press** the number of the floor you want to go to.
> To glue two pieces of wood together, you must put glue on one
>   piece and then **press** the two pieces together for several minutes.

(b) [a machine for printing newspapers and magazines]

> My brother works for the city newspaper; he operates the printing
>   **presses**.

(c) [printed media]

> The **press** in some countries is free to print opinions against the
>   government. But in some countries the **press** is restricted by the
>   government.

15. urban [characteristic of a city; having to do with a city]

> I live in the middle of a city because I prefer **urban** to rural areas.
> A typical **urban** family in the United States has two cars and likes
>   entertainment such as theater, ballet, and movies.

16. steep (a) [almost straight up and down, such as a mountain or a road]

> The road up the mountain was too **steep**; my car would not go
>   up it.
> The university is on the top of a **steep** hill. It is too difficult for me
>   to walk up it.

(b) {informal} [too expensive]

> I did not buy the four-door car because the price was too **steep**. The
>   two-door car was much cheaper.

> A: I want to travel to Washington, D.C. Which is cheaper, going by
>   plane or by train?
> B: Going by a plane is probably cheaper. The cost of train travel is
>   quite **steep** in this country.

17. tip (a) [money paid for service, for example, at a restaurant]

> At a restaurant in the United States, the custom is to leave a **tip** of
>   fifteen percent of the cost of the meal on the table.

> A: How much should I **tip** a taxi-driver?
> B: About fifteen percent of the cost of the ride.

(b) [the end of something]

> The **tip** of a pencil is sharp—do not put it near your eyes.
> For safety, you should cover the **tip** of a pole or anything sharp with
>   a piece of rubber.

Introductory Exercises

A. Match each word with its definition.

    ____ **1.** a large, important road

    ____ **2.** to rub your skin

    ____ **3.** the end of something

    ____ **4.** to stop or slow down

    ____ **5.** a part of a machine that is pushed by the foot

    ____ **6.** related to cities

    ____ **7.** a small hole

    ____ **8.** to pull slowly

    ____ **9.** to move your head up and down

    ____ **10.** although

    ____ **11.** to push on something

    ____ **12.** to make something expanded and better

    ____ **13.** anything carried by a train or truck

a. brake
b. dent
c. despite
d. develop
e. drag
f. freight
g. highway
h. nod
i. pedal
j. platform
k. press
l. roll
m. scratch
n. steep
o. tip
p. urban

B. Answer **TRUE** or **FALSE**.

1. When an American disagrees with you, he nods his head.
2. If you scratch a car, you will leave a mark.
3. Some musical instruments have pedals.
4. Farmers grow crops in urban areas.
5. Bicycles have brakes.
6. A ball will roll by itself down a steep hill.
7. Americans usually leave a five percent tip in restaurants.
8. People can carry heavy freight on a small bicycle.
9. You can often have pictures developed at a camera shop.
10. People must drive as fast as possible on all highways.
11. Despite the high prices, New York is visited by many tourists.
12. The press is responsible for news in the newspaper.

Study Exercises

C. In the blanks, write the appropriate word(s) from the word form chart in this unit.

1. At the airport you often see people _____ suitcases that are too heavy to carry.

2. If you _____ on the brakes too fast on a wet road, your car will slide.

3. It's difficult to bicycle up a(n) _____ hill.

4. On our vacation we traveled on a highway that ran _____ a river. The view was fantastic.

5. My grandmother has a beautiful wooden desk. It's a hundred years old, but it's in excellent condition. It doesn't have a(n) _____ on it.

6. Last weekend at the train station I saw a child almost fall off the _____ , but fortunately he was saved by a young man.

7. I stayed up late to watch a movie last night, _____ the fact that I had only slept three hours the night before.

8. Some cars have two _____ —one for gas and one for brakes—but some have three.

9. The handle of one of my cups broke, so I repaired it by putting glue on the handle and _____ it to the cup for about ten minutes.

10. A student's foreign language ability can only _____ if the student studies and practices with native speakers of that language.

11. Children should be careful with pencils because their _____ can be very sharp.

12. The teacher told the students to _____ their heads if they understood what she was saying.

D. Write a short answer for these questions. Use a word from the word form chart.

1. What happens to your car if you hit a telephone pole? _____

_____

2. What kind of road is dangerous to drive on in the snow? _____

_____

3. In what type of area do you find big buildings, shops, and

apartments? _____

_____

4. What do trains and trucks both carry? _____

_____

5. What might an angry cat do to a dog? _____

_____

6. What happens to an orange if you put it on a table and then lift up

the table? _____

_____

7. What is a fast way to travel from one city to another? _____

_____

8. What should you do if you're driving on the highway and the car in

front of you stops suddenly? _____

_____

9. What do Americans do after they pay the bill in a restaurant? _____

_____

10. What happens when people fall asleep in class? _____

_____

11. What is another word for "riding a bicycle"? _____

_____

12. What might you do if you are going to a party, and your cousin

comes to visit unexpectedly from out of town? _____

_____

E. Match each word with its opposite.

_____ 1. drag   **a.** gas pedal
_____ 2. develop   **b.** because of
                       c. shake
_____ 3. despite   **d.** city street
_____ 4. brake pedal   **e.** middle
_____ 5. highway   **f.** rural
                       g. push
_____ 6. nod (your head) **h.** destroy
_____ 7. tip
_____ 8. urban

F. Read the passage, an article from a newspaper, and answer the questions that follow.

UNUSUAL ACCIDENT ENDS WELL

Yesterday evening around 10:00, an unusual accident occurred at the intersection of Highway 81 and Ulmerton Road. A freight truck carrying a load of hay was driving along
5 Highway 81; the driver of the truck had been driving since 5:00 A.M. Because he was so tired, his head began to nod, and he started to fall asleep at the point where Highway 81 goes down a steep hill. He woke up as the truck rolled downhill and immediately pressed the brake pedal. However, the
10 brakes did not work, and the truck continued to roll down the hill. At the bottom of the hill is Ulmerton Road. As the truck rolled through the intersection, another truck with a load of horses was crossing it. The back end of the hay truck caught the tip of the end of the horse truck and dragged it
15 about 500 feet. Both trucks came to rest in a field along the highway. Half of the hay had fallen out of the truck, and the door of the horse truck had a large dent and fell off. By the time both drivers got out of their trucks, the horses were all eating the hay that had spilled. Despite the speed and size of
20 the trucks, neither the drivers nor the horses had a scratch on them. And fortunately for everyone, the accident did not happen in the middle of an urban development—in the country the trucks had a soft field to land in.

1. When did the accident happen? _____

_____

2. How long had the first driver been driving? _____

_____

3. What kind of freight did the first truck have? The second truck? _____

_____

4. Why didn't the hay truck stop before the intersection? _____

_____

5. How far did the first truck drag the second truck? _____

_____

6. Describe the damage to the trucks. _____

_____

7. What happened to the hay? _____

_____

8. What happened to the horses? _____

_____

9. Where did the accident take place? _____

_____

Follow-up

G. Dictation: Write the sentences that your teacher reads aloud.

1. _____

2. _____

3. _____

4. _____

5. _____

H. Answer the following questions.

1. What kind of freight do trains or trucks carry in your country?
2. Describe the highway system in your country.
3. What are the important highways near the city where you are living? What other cities do they go to?
4. Do people leave a tip in restaurants in your country? How much?
5. Where do you take film for developing?
6. What does it mean to nod your head in your country?
7. Describe the relationship between the press and the government in your country.
8. What is your opinion of the press in the United States?
9. What should you do if you scratch yourself on an old nail?
10. Tell why you prefer to live in an urban or a rural area.

I.
1. Describe the transportation system in your country.
2. Describe an accident that you have seen or that you have been in.

Work (B)

Word Form Chart

NOUN	VERB	ADJECTIVE	ADVERB
attainment	attain	attainable	
		unattainable	
		blue-collar	
expression	express	expressive	expressively
flaw		flawed	
goal			
incentive			
jewel			
jewelry			
leisure		leisure	
		leisurely	leisurely
manual		manual	manually
pension		pension	
pensioner			
plant			
potential		potential	potentially
presentation	present	presented	
		presenting	
raw materials			
section	section	sectional	
task			
waiter	wait on		
waitress			
		white-collar	

Definitions and Examples

1. **plant** (a) [a factory]

    My grandfather worked at the auto **plant** for 40 years.
    Because the demand for steel fell, all the **plants** in the area have
      shut down.

    (b) [1:19: A living thing that is not an animal]

      There were many **plants** in the garden, including unusual
        flowers and trees.

2. **manual** (a) [of or with the hands; using human energy instead of
   machines]

    Manual labor is physically very demanding.
    Deaf people use a **manual** alphabet to communicate; in other
      words, they give signals with their hands.

   (b) [any type of book which gives instructions]

    The stereo came with an operation and repair **manual**.
    We read the whole owner's **manual** before we decided to buy
      the car.

3. **blue-collar** [having to do with manual laborers]

    Farmers, truck drivers, and building construction workers are all
      examples of **blue-collar** workers.

4. **white-collar** [having to do with professional work requiring an
   educational degree]

    Teachers, business executives, doctors, and lawyers are examples of
      white-collar workers.

5. **section** [a part of something; to divide into parts]

    We could not find the **section** of the manual that we needed.
    The plant employs 50 blue-collar and six white-collar workers in its
      assembly **section**.
    They **sectioned** the room into four different work areas.

6. **task** [a piece of assigned work]

    The secretary had to finish three **tasks**, one of which was to type a
      letter.
    He quit his job because of all the extra **tasks** he had to do without
      pay.

7. **quarrel** [to argue angrily; an angry argument; a reason for argument]

   They **quarreled** for over an hour about who was responsible for the mistake.

   A: What is your **quarrel** with the way the plant is being run?
   B: We don't like how the management keeps hiring friends who are not qualified.

8. **leisure** [free time; convenience; free from compulsory activity]

   Please feel free to visit our office at your **leisure**.
   We spent a **leisurely** afternoon in the park.
   Sports can be interesting **leisure** activities.

9. **flaw** [an imperfection; a defeat; a weakness]

   There was a **flaw** in the surface of the glass.
   His character has many **flaws**.
   The key **flaw** in our company is the lack of qualified management personnel.

10. **jewel** [a precious stone]

    Kings and queens usually own many **jewels**.
    The **jewels** were guarded very heavily while they were shown at the museum.

11. **jewelry** [anything made of metal, stone, plastic, etc., worn on the wrist, finger, ears, or around the neck, etc.]

    She wore all her diamond **jewelry** to the party.
    The thieves stole only the expensive **jewelry**; they left all the worthless **jewelry** alone.

12. **incentive** [anything which makes a person want to make an effort]

    A pay raise is usually an **incentive** to work harder.
    Fear of losing your job is also an **incentive** for doing good work.
    Not having money for clothes is **incentive** for learning how to sew.

13. **waiter** [a man who serves food in a restaurant]

    The **waiter** took our order and shortly returned with our meal.
    The **waiter** was so impolite that we did not leave him a tip.

14. **potential** [something possible but not yet used]

    She has a lot of **potential** ability for leadership but has not had the opportunity to develop.
    With all the electrical problems in the plant, there is great **potential** for fire.

15. **goal** [anything that you work toward; a final purpose]

> His career **goal** is to become a doctor.
> Our **goal** is to teach the employees to identify potential problems with the machinery.

16. **attain** [to accomplish; to reach; to arrive at]

> You must work hard to **attain** your goals.
> He **attained** the age of 84.

17. **raw material** [the materials not yet developed into products that can be sold]

> Wood is one of the **raw materials** used in making paper.
> Cotton and wool are two **raw materials** the plant buys to make fabric.

18. **pension** [an amount of money paid regularly, especially as a retirement benefit]

> As soon as my father retired from his job, he began to receive a **pension** once a month.
> We receive our **pension** checks at the beginning of every month.

19. **present** (with) (a) [to introduce; to bring before the public; to give]

> He **presented** his wife to everyone at the dinner.
> The company **presented** its views on a national television program.
> When he retired, the company **presented** him with a gold watch.

> (b) [1-16: now; at this time]

>> The **present** problem with pollution is very bad.

20. **express** [to communicate an idea, emotion, etc., especially by words]

> It is often difficult to **express** your exact ideas in another language.
> He **expressed** his anger by hitting the desk with his hand.

21. **expression** (a) [the communication of an idea; a word or group of words]

> Marianne's **expression** of her disapproval surprised everyone.
> We learned a lot of new **expressions** when we went to Spain.

(b) [the look on a person's face when under certain emotions]

> You could see that Mary was surprised by the **expression** on her face.
> Melodie's final **expression** told us she was worried.

Introductory Exercises

A. Match each word with its definition.

_____ **1.** a part or piece of something
_____ **2.** possibility
_____ **3.** a small job you have to do
_____ **4.** free time
_____ **5.** with the hands
_____ **6.** using a lot of emotion when communicating
_____ **7.** a man who serves food
_____ **8.** something you work toward
_____ **9.** not perfect
_____ **10.** a factory

a. attainable
b. expressive
c. flawed
d. goal
e. incentive
f. leisure
g. manually
h. pension
i. plant
j. presentation
k. section
l. task
m. waiter

B. Complete the following statements.

1. If a glass has a small break in it, it has a(n) _____ .

2. Washing the dishes is an example of a small _____ .

3. If you need directions on how to do something, you can look in a(n) _____ .

4. If you don't like cigarettes, you should sit in the no-smoking _____ .

5. Trees, metals, wool, diamonds, and other jewels are all examples of _____ .

6. Many people when they retire receive a(n) _____ .

7. A goal that you cannot reach is _____ .

8. Giving a talk and showing pictures are parts of a(n) _____ .

9. If something has a lot of possible uses, it has great _____ .

10. Another name for a factory is a(n) _____ .

11. Workers with a university education are called _____ .

12. Workers such as construction workers are _____ .

Study Exercises

C. In the blanks, write the appropriate word from the word form chart.

1. to state your ideas
2. a restaurant worker
3. a part of something
4. a restful time
5. pretty things to wear, usually of metal
6. having to do with the hands
7. possible uses for something
8. having something wrong
9. a reason for doing something
10. to accomplish something
11. something you try to accomplish
12. to give a talk, a gift, etc.

1. — — □ — — — — —
2. — — — — □ — — —
3. — □ — — — — — —
4. — — — □ — — — —
5. — — — □ — — —
6. — — □ — — —
7. — — □ — — — — — —
8. — — □ — — —
9. — — — — — □ — — —
10. — — — — □ — —
11. — □ — —
12. — — — — — □ —

13. (a) What word is spelled in the boxes above?
    (b) What does this word mean? Give three examples.

D. In the blanks, write the appropriate word(s) from the word form chart in this unit.

1. Industry uses many _____ in manufacturing products.
2. We _____ 30 tables at the restaurant last night.
3. An orange can easily be separated into its _____ .
4. I like to read and relax during my _____ time.
5. The _____ manager is responsible for the operations of the entire factory.
6. More money and a greater challenge are two _____ for changing jobs.
7. A small hole in a fabric, or a break at the edge of a plate, is a(n) _____ .
8. Their _____ for the future is to develop the raw materials to their fullest potential.
9. We don't have a machine to cut the vegetables; we have to do it _____ .
10. "Ouch!" is a word which _____ pain.

E. Write **T** if the sentence is true and **F** if it is false.

____ 1. You receive a pension at age fifteen.
____ 2. If you want to know how to maintain your car, you should read the owner's manual.
____ 3. A leisurely task is a very difficult one.
____ 4. A goal is anything that you try to attain.
____ 5. Many people have flaws in their skin.
____ 6. A truck driver is a white-collar worker.
____ 7. A person who has potential will definitely use it.
____ 8. You can frequently tell what a person is thinking by the expression on his face.
____ 9. Snow can create potentially dangerous driving conditions.
____ 10. If you set very high goals, it may be difficult to attain them.

F. Read the passage and answer the questions that follow.

In our town, the main source of income is the jewelry industry. We are very fortunate to be located in an area of the country that has plenty of raw materials used in

manufacturing jewelry. There are many gold and silver mines
5   as well as a number of mines that produce diamonds and
other jewels.

Most of the townspeople are employed at one of three
jewelry plants. Both white-collar and blue-collar workers
have jobs at the plants, but they have different
10   responsibilities. The white-collar workers, for example, are
responsible for the business and development aspects of the
plant. They work in the offices and take care of paying bills
and arranging sales locally and abroad. They also organize
meetings and prepare presentations for jewelry stores to
15   announce new styles and prices of jewelry.

While the office workers work with the business end of
the plant, the blue-collar employees work directly with the
manufacture of the jewelry. The plant generally can be
broken down into two basic sections, the first of which is the
20   department where jewels are cut into the appropriate shape.
The workers there must be very skilled because the slightest
mistake when cutting a diamond or other jewel could create
a flaw which would reduce the value of the stone. Cutting
the jewels is a very important task in the process of jewelry
25   making. Because it is so important, the jewel cutters are
given a lot of leisure time throughout the day so that they
are mentally prepared to make each cut.

In another section of the plant, the people have the task
of forming the metals into the proper shape. They must heat
30   the metals until they attain a certain temperature before they
can begin the shaping process. Once they have achieved the
correct shape, they make sure that all edges of the jewelry
are smooth, and then they set the stones securely in place.
When they have finished this step, they carefully polish each
35   piece of jewelry and send it to the section of the plant
responsible for wrapping and packaging each item.

The jewelry from our town is extremely expensive, but
there are a number of good reasons for this fact. First of all,
the plants use only the highest quality raw materials in their
40   jewelry. Also, all of the workers are very highly skilled, but
most importantly, each step of the manufacturing process is
done manually. Each piece of jewelry is made separately with
the personal attention of the workers, so the buyer can be
assured that the jewelry will contain no flaws.

1. Why is the jewelry industry the main source of income? _____

_____

2. What is the difference between the white-collar workers and the

blue-collar workers? _____

_____

3. How does the plant inform the public of its new styles and

   prices? _____

   _____

4. What two sections make up the plants? _____

   _____

5. Why do the workers in the first section of the plant have to be very

   careful? _____

   _____

6. What do the plant managers do to try to reduce mistakes in this

   department? _____

   _____

7. Why is the jewelry manufactured in this town so expensive? _____

   _____

Follow-up

G. Dictation: Write the sentences that your teacher reads aloud.

   1. _____

   2. _____

   3. _____

   4. _____

   5. _____

H. Give a synonym for the underlined word or words.

   1. You can't go into the next level until you <u>achieve</u> good
      grades. _____

   2. The president generally <u>states</u> his ideas very clearly and
      directly. _____

3. There was <u>something wrong</u> in the design of his sweater.

    _____

4. My <u>plan</u> is to finish school by December and find a job.

    _____

5. He has a lot of <u>reasons</u> for losing weight. _____

6. He took a <u>nice, easy</u> bicycle ride around the farm. _____

7. This town has <u>many possibilities</u>. _____

8. This book has three different <u>groups</u> of exercises. _____

9. Her job consists of many different <u>things to do</u>. _____

10. They will have six <u>food servers</u> at the party. _____

I. Answer the following questions.

1. What section of the city do you live in?
2. What incentives do you have for staying in that section of the city?
3. What is your primary goal for the near future? For the distant future?
4. What was one of the most difficult goals you have attained in the past? What made it so difficult? What were your incentives?
5. Do you consider yourself an expressive person? Why? Why not?
6. Do you enjoy giving presentations in front of large groups? Why? Why not? What is the most recent presentation you have given? Was it successful? How do you know?
7. What is the most boring task you were ever asked to do? What was your incentive for completing the task?
8. What do you feel is your greatest potential? How do you plan to develop this potential?
9. Have you ever waited on tables in a restaurant? If you have, what was your worst experience in that job? Your most memorable?
10. Does your country/company/business have a pension plan for its employees? If so, describe it. If not, what do the people do instead?

Answer Key

Unit 1

C. 1. T 2. F 3. T 4. T 5. F 6. F 7. T 8. T 9. T 10. F

D. 1. patience/knowledge/cleverness 2. advisor 3. orientation
4. equipment 5. attitude 6. knowledge 7. confusing 8. records

E. 1. My advisor told me to take chemistry. 2. That professor is fair to most of
his students. 3. English is not optional, but physics is. 4. The textbook is
confusing, and I am confused. 5. She is impatient to take intermediate level
chemistry. 6. He looked neat the first day of school./The first day of school
he looked neat.

F. 1. long before they graduate from high school 2. They take special
courses. 3. They send an application and their student record. 4. yes
5. Orientation teaches students procedures for registration and student
advising, university rules, the use of the library, and other major services of
the college or university. 6. other new students, some professors, and some
university administrators

Unit 2

C. 1. T 2. F 3. T 4. F 5. T 6. T 7. T 8. T 9. F 10. T

D. 1. c 2. i 3. a 4. b 5. d 6. h 7. f 8. j

E. 1. bend 2. pilot 3. fare 4. connection 5. main 6. divide 7. iron

F. 1. the main road connecting the country's two largest cities 2. an iron
divider 3. Several of the worst bends in the road will be reconstructed. 4. to
make the road safer 5. if people drove more carefully

Unit 3

C. 1. F 2. T 3. F 4. F 5. T 6. F 7. T 8. F 9. F 10. F

D. 1. c 2. i 3. a 4. f 5. d 6. e 7. f

E. 1. exports 2. department 3. output 4. appointed/promoted
5. gradually 6. partners 7. personnel 8. retire 9. incomes 10. ladder

F. 1. to the personnel department 2. That was the time of his appointment.
3. the applicants' college grades and previous work experience 4. an increase
in income for each promotion and a good retirement program 5. a major
export project

Unit 4

C. 1. F 2. F 3. F 4. T 5. F 6. F 7. T 8. T 9. T 10. T

D. I. 1. tense 2. luxury 3. primitive 4. plain 5. flexible
II. 1. pioneer 2. flex 3. extend 4. echo 5. occupy

E. 1. extended 2. primitive 3. tent 4. canvas 5. adjust 6. luxurious
7. flexible 8. tense

Unit 5

C. 1. F 2. F 3. T 4. T 5. F 6. F 7. T 8. F 9. F 10. T 11. F

D. 1. journalism 2. reputation 3. illustrate 4. significant 5. suggestions
6. compare 7. issue 8. implies 9. list 10. index

E. 1. compromise 2. fair 3. adequate 4. issue 5. sudden 6. personnel
7. title 8. break

F. ACROSS: 1. insignificant 6. index 8. reporters 9. illustrated
10. journalist 11. list 12. constant
DOWN: 2. suggested 3. comparisons 4. fold 5. editorial
6. implication 7. quote 8. reputation

Unit 6

C. 1. T 2. F 3. F 4. F 5. T 6. T 7. T 8. F 9. T 10. F

D. 1. drowned 2. recovered 3. diagnosis 4. epidemic 5. consult 6. tiny
7. fainted 8. chart 9. crazy 10. lungs.

F. 1. cancer 2. (a) She had severe pains in her belly for three weeks. (b) She lost
all her energy. 3. He found her unconscious. 4. a simple stomach
infection 5. one week 6. her delay in consulting a doctor for so long

Unit 7

C. 1. F 2. T 3. T 4. F 5. T 6. T 7. F 8. F 9. T 10. T

D. 1. antique 2. gray 3. carpenter 4. maintain 5. shelter 6. help
7. furnace 8. draw

E. 1. gray 2. district 3. cabinet 4. adequate 5. bulb 6. shelter 7. drew
8. inherit 9. hammer 10. maintenance

F. 1. They inherited twenty thousand dollars from Mary's grandmother. 2. in
various districts of the city 3. because it had not been maintained
adequately 4. a group of carpenters 5. the constant hammering of the
carpenters

Unit 8

C. 1. T 2. T 3. T 4. F 5. F 6. F 7. T 8. F 9. F

D. 1. Rain is extremely unlikely. 2. Radar helps us to forecast the weather. 3. A sheet of ice covered the ground. 4. Today is noticeably colder than yesterday. 5. I didn't notice the change in the weather. 6. It snowed steadily for two hours. 7. At dawn, the peninsula suffered an earthquake./The peninsula suffered an earthquake at dawn. 8. The range of temperature is extreme.

E. 1. dawn 2. remind 3. peninsula 4. mild 5. soft 6. suffer 7. range 8. sun 9. slow

F. 1. mild, often cool and wet 2. sweaters and jackets 3. The weather is softened by the relatively warm air and water of the Pacific Ocean. 4. The weather outside the city is much warmer and drier. 5. earthquakes 6. a powerful earthquake 7. by storing large amounts of food and other necessities and constructing houses and buildings that can bear the stress produced by earthquakes 8. No place is 100% safe.

Unit 9

C. 1. F 2. F 3. T 4. T 5. T 6. F 7. T 8. F 9. F 10. T

D. 1. j 2. f 3. a 4. g 5. b 6. c 7. h 8. d

E. 1. beneath 2. introduced 3. technique 4. ashamed 5. definitely/awfully 6. demonstrations 7. eliminate 8. disgusting

F. 1. a demonstration, because of the company's recent announcement of its new technique for mining diamonds 2. American conservationists, because they feel that this new method of mining will leave the area unfit for wildlife 3. They feel the damage will last less than twenty years after the end of the mining operation. 4. large areas of forest 5. wildlife

Unit 10

C. 1. T 2. F 3. F 4. T 5. T 6. F 7. T 8. T 9. F

D. 1. attractive/feminine 2. aware 3. button 4. polish 5. worn out 6. pin/ needle 7. patterned 8. shrinking

E. 1. atmosphere 2. deposit 3. exchange 4. traditional 5. worn out 6. shrunken 7. powder 8. dyed

F. 1. F 2. F 3. T 4. F 5. T 6. F 7. F 8. F 9. F

Unit 11

C. 1. F 2. T 3. F 4. F 5. T 6. F 7. F 8. T 9. T 10. F 11. F

D. 1. resources 2. herd, crisis 3. fertilizer 4. pipes 5. settled 6. circumstances 7. tied 8. crisis 9. enormous

E. 1. Farmers had been producing enormous quantities of crops, and their products had become too plentiful inside the United States. 2. It rose. 3. There was usually enough rain. 4. The grass became dry and brown. 5. They had to sell all their possessions to pay their bills. 6. Some farmers in other areas had a prosperous year.

Unit 12

C. **1.** c **2.** j **3.** e **4.** a **5.** g **6.** d **7.** b **8.** i **9.** f **10.** h

D. **1.** agent **2.** document **3.** benefits **4.** protesters **5.** trade **6.** aid
7. established **8.** authority **9.** balance **10.** stable **11.** immigration
12. insistent

E. **1.** foreign people who want to settle permanently in the United States
2. guarding a United States border or processing immigration documents **3.** to
benefit all of the United States society by balancing the number of immigrants
from each country **4.** They recognize that the talents and skills of many
immigrants have helped the country progress, and they want to aid
immigrants' search for a new life.

Unit 13

C. **1.** F **2.** T **3.** F **4.** F **5.** T **6.** T **7.** T **8.** T **9.** T **10.** T **11.** T **12.** F

D. **1.** c **2.** e **3.** i **4.** m **5.** a **6.** g **7.** f **8.** k **9.** h **10.** b **11.** d

E. **1.** cubes **2.** classified **3.** cracked **4.** mankind **5.** Minus **6.** cement
7. isolated **8.** illumination **9.** circumference **10.** atomic **11.** three-
dimensional **12.** rotation

Unit 14

C. **1.** T **2.** F **3.** T **4.** T **5.** F **6.** T **7.** F **8.** T **9.** F **10.** T

D. **1.** series **2.** out of stock **3.** scheme **4.** willing **5.** tend **6.** specify
7. merchandise **8.** sum **9.** Ultimately **10.** nearly/ultimately/quickly/
willingly

E. **1.** approve **2.** humid **3.** foolish **4.** severe **5.** residence **6.** expert
7. formal **8.** classify **9.** cruel **10.** secret

F. **1.** to be a neighborhood grocer **2.** yes **3.** He was willing to work long hours,
and his store sold a wide range of merchandise. **4.** small things, like having
correct labels **5.** improvements in his store **6.** A series of floods caused
many foods to be out of stock for weeks. **7.** my grandfather

Unit 15

C. **1.** e **2.** a **3.** d **4.** f **5.** b

D. **1.** bribe **2.** doubt **3.** chased **4.** identified **5.** conscience **6.** alarm
7. cell **8.** confession **9.** fake **10.** hide

E. **1.** two months **2.** They chased him in their car. No. **3.** in an inside pocket
of his jacket **4.** The owner identified them. **5.** Yes, they have no doubt.
6. alarmed

Unit 16

C. **1.** bitter **2.** raw **3.** lambs **4.** cream **5.** tongue **6.** shook **7.** contents
8. nuts **9.** basket **10.** swells **11.** was pouring **12.** brand **13.** stir

D. **1.** h **2.** a **3.** f **4.** i **5.** e **6.** b

E. **1.** alcohol   **2.** assemble   **3.** stir/shake   **4.** contents   **5.** swollen   **6.** brand
7. dairy   **8.** contents   **9.** baskets   **10.** nuts   **11.** assembles

Unit 17

C. **1.** e   **2.** a   **3.** d   **4.** h   **5.** g   **6.** b   **7.** f   **8.** c

D. **1.** c   **2.** f   **3.** a   **4.** g   **5.** d   **6.** e   **7.** b

E. **1.** obey   **2.** gained   **3.** eventful/stupid/giant   **4.** operation   **5.** rope
6. memorize   **7.** target   **8.** occurred   **9.** concern   **10.** considerable

F. **1.** three weeks   **2.** the necessity of the yearly "war games"   **3.** to insure that
the soldiers have gained the fighting skills required for battle   **4.** hitting
targets and memorizing maps   **5.** obedience and courage   **6.** They think it is
stupid to invent a warlike situation, and the yearly event usually results in
injuries to some of the soldiers.

Unit 18

C. **1.** F   **2.** F   **3.** T   **4.** T   **5.** T   **6.** F   **7.** F   **8.** T   **9.** T   **10.** F

D. **1.** permission   **2.** ancestors   **3.** caring for   **4.** elderly   **5.** widowed   **6.** bring
up   **7.** delighted/encouraged   **8.** encouraging   **9.** accompany   **10.** discouraged
11. companion

E. **1.** alone   **2.** the "selfishness" of the younger generation   **3.** in the
surroundings that they are familiar with   **4.** a very positive influence
5. (a) They live longer. (b) They are healthier, (c) They have better attitudes
toward life.

Unit 19

C. **1.** F   **2.** F   **3.** T   **4.** F   **5.** T   **6.** F   **7.** T   **8.** T   **9.** T   **10.** T

D. **1.** nest   **2.** gather, sticks   **3.** feed on   **4.** remain   **5.** rescue   **6.** roughly
7. wings   **8.** spills   **9.** bank   **10.** bay   **11.** create

E. **1.** go   **2.** shell   **3.** food   **4.** gather   **5.** banks   **6.** rescue   **7.** remain   **8.** stick
9. shell

F. **1.** F   **2.** T   **3.** T   **4.** T   **5.** T   **6.** T   **7.** F
8. pink   **9.** She rescues them.   **10.** by gathering and organizing sticks, grass,
and feathers   **11.** She replaces them.   **12.** their wings

Unit 20

C. **1.** T   **2.** T   **3.** F   **4.** T   **5.** T   **6.** T   **7.** F   **8.** T   **9.** F   **10.** F

D. **1.** blessing   **2.** mortal   **3.** decorated   **4.** Sacred   **5.** robe   **6.** worship
7. amazing   **8.** funeral   **9.** preacher/priest/priestess   **10.** Lord

E. **1.** assigned   **2.** accustomed to   **3.** talent   **4.** Mr.   **5.** hell   **6.** enormous
7. profit   **8.** amateur

F. **1.** how hard priests work and how busy their days are   **2.** the spiritual lives of
the people they are close to   **3.** say the blessings   **4.** priests   **5.** good, evil, and
immortality   **6.** during the holiday season   **7.** a beautiful robe   **8.** because he
is a servant of the Lord

Unit 21

C. **1.** whole **2.** Challenging **3.** grab **4.** position **5.** postponed **6.** routine **7.** waved **8.** obstacle **9.** temper **10.** rubbed **11.** cycle

D. **1.** whole **2.** point **3.** volleyball **4.** league **5.** position **6.** obstacle **7.** temper **8.** muscular **9.** routine **10.** grab **11.** cycling **12.** challenging **13.** aspect **14.** tire **15.** postpone **16.** wave **17.** rub

E. **1.** They spend too much time on their sports and not enough on their classes. **2.** physical, emotional, and social **3.** An athlete makes his muscles stronger and increases the capacity of his heart and lungs. **4.** You don't get as tired, eat less, and have more energy. **5.** You learn to control your temper. **6.** You learn to cooperate with others, accept challenges, face obstacles, make good decisions, and organize your time wisely. In general, you gain confidence in many areas.

Unit 22

C. **1.** F **2.** T **3.** F **4.** T **5.** F **6.** F **7.** F **8.** T **9.** F **10.** T **11.** T

D. **1.** deduct **2.** loan **3.** asset **4.** gamble **5.** matter **6.** term **7.** rude **8.** deadline **9.** deduce

E. **1.** 40% **2.** bank balances and buildings and equipment **3.** that 70% of their employees will be natives of this country **4.** They have protested that investment should not be controlled by the government. **5.** F **6.** T **7.** T **8.** F **9.** F **10.** T

Unit 23

C. **1.** marks **2.** pace **3.** master **4.** theoretical **5.** capable **6.** beyond **7.** assumed **8.** chief **9.** rejected **10.** conference **11.** essay **12.** theory/ concept/assumption **13.** philosophies/civilizations

D. **1.** F **2.** F **3.** T **4.** F **5.** T **6.** T **7.** F **8.** F **9.** F **10.** F

E. **1.** mark **2.** greeting **3.** conference **4.** chief **5.** comment **6.** pace **7.** theoretical **8.** chair **9.** assume **10.** win

F. **1.** to possible new students, because they have expressed an interest in Brackster College **2.** students with a good foundation in science, math, history, and English who are able to express themselves clearly **3.** academic ability, honesty, and moral character **4.** to think critically and make intelligent decisions **5.** to see if they can express themselves clearly **6.** a wide variety of careers rather than specific careers **7.** Students can succeed in a wide variety of careers and can change careers without difficulty. **8.** They are not prepared for specific careers. **9.** There are mountains, and it snows in the winter.

Unit 24

C. **1.** dragging/rolling **2.** press **3.** steep **4.** along **5.** scratch **6.** platform **7.** despite **8.** pedals **9.** pressing **10.** develop **11.** tips **12.** nod

D. **1.** You will dent your car. **2.** a steep road **3.** an urban or developed area **7.** freight **8.** scratch it **9.** It rolls off. **10.** on a highway **11.** Use your brake. **12.** leave a tip **13.** They nod their heads. **14.** pedaling **15.** Take your cousin along.

E. **1.** g **2.** h **3.** b **4.** a **5.** d **6.** c **7.** e **8.** f

F. **1.** yesterday evening around 10:00 **2.** since 5:00 a.m. **3.** hay, horses **4.** The brakes didn't work. **5.** 500 feet **6.** The door of the horse truck had a large dent and fell off, but the hay truck was not damaged. **7.** Half of the hay fell out of the truck and was eaten by the horses. **8.** They got out of the truck, but they were not injured. **9.** at the intersection of Highway 81 and Ulmerton Road

Unit 25

C. **1.** express **2.** waitress **3.** section **4.** leisure **5.** jewelry **6.** manual **7.** potential **8.** flawed **9.** incentive **10.** attain **11.** goal **12.** present **13.** (a) PRESENTATION (b) anything you give publicly; for example, a speech, a play, or a prize

D. **1.** raw materials **2.** waited on **3.** sections **4.** leisure **5.** plant **6.** incentives **7.** flaw **8.** goal **9.** manually **10.** expresses

E. **1.** F **2.** T **3.** F **4.** T **5.** T **6.** F **7.** F **8.** T **9.** T **10.** T

F. **1.** because the area has plenty of the raw materials used in manufacturing jewelry **2.** The white-collar workers are responsible for the business and development aspects of the plant. The blue-collar workers manufacture the jewelry. **3.** The white-collar workers organize meetings and presentations for the jewelry stores. **4.** One section cuts the jewels, and the other forms the metals. **5.** If the workers make a mistake, they could ruin the jewel. **6.** They permit the workers to have a lot of leisure time. **7.** They use only the best raw materials, do the work manually, and make each piece separately.

Words Assumed for Volume 1

a	at	book	clean	difficult
able	August	born	clock	dinner
about	aunt	both	clothes	dirty
absent		box	clothing	do
after		boy	coat	doctor
again	baby	bread	coffee	dog
age	bad	breakfast	cold	dollar
ago	ball	bring	color	door
air	bank	brother	come	dormitory
all	bath	brown	complete	down
almost	be (am, is,	build	continue	dream
already	are, was,	(built)	cook	drink
also	were, been)	busy	corner	drive
always	beautiful	but	correct	during
an	because	buy	cost	
and	become	(bought)	could	
animal	bed	by	country	each
another	before		cousin	ear
answer	begin		cow	east
any	beside	call	cry	easy
anybody	best	can	cup	eat
anyone	better	can't	cut	egg
anything	between	car		eight
anywhere	big	cat		elephant
apple	bird	centimeter	dance	eleven
April	black	chair	dark	end
are	blackboard	chicken	daughter	enough
arm	blood	child	day	enter
arms	blue	(children)	dead	etc. (etcetera)
arrive	board	church	December	cvery
as	boat	city	desk	explain
ask	bone	class	different	eye

February
Friday
face
fall (n)
false
family
famous
far
fast
fat
father
feel
feet
female
few
fifth
find
fine
finger
finish
fire
first
fish
five
flag
floor
flower
fly
food
foot
  (feet)
forget
forth
forty
four
free
friend
from
front
fruit
future

garden
get
gift
girl
give
go
gold
good
good-bye

gram
grandfather
grandmother
grass
green

hair
half
hand
handsome
happy
hat
have
have to
he
head
hear
help
her
herself
here
high
him
himself
his
hit
hold
holiday
home
hope
horse
hospital
hot
hotel
hour
house
how
hundred
husband

I
ice
idea
if
important
in
inside
interest
into
is

it
its
itself

job

key
kilogram
kilometer
king
kiss
kitchen
knife
know

lady
land
language
large
last (adj)
late
laugh
learn
left
leg
lesson
letter
library
life
like
listen
little
live
long
look
a lot of
love
lunch

Miss
Mr.
Mrs.
machine
magazine
mail
make
  (made)
male

man (men)
many
map
marry
may
maybe
me
mean (v)
meat
medicine
meet
meter
might
milk
million
minute
mistake
money
month
moon
more
morning
most
mother
mountain
mouth
move
movies
much
music
must
my
myself

name
near
necessary
need
neighbor
never
new
news
newspaper
next
nice
night
nine
no
nobody
noise
none

no one
(no-one)
  north
nose
not
nothing
now
nowhere
number

ocean
o'clock
of
off
office
often
old
on
once
one
only
open
or
other
our
ours
ourselves
out
over

page
paper
parent
part
party
past
pay
peace
pen
pencil
permit
person
  (people)
picture
plane
play
please
police
poor
practice

pretty	ship	stand	this	warm
price	shirt	start	those	wash
problem	shoe	stone	thousand	watch
put	shop	stop	three	water
	short	story	throw	way
	should	street	time	we
queen	show	strong	today	weather
question	shut	student	tomorrow	week
quiet	sick	study	tonight	well
	side	subject	too	west
	sing	such	tooth	what
radio	sister	sugar	top	when
railroad	sit	summer	train	where
rain	six	sun	tree	which
read	sleep	swim	true	white
red	slow		try	who
remember	small		twelve	whom
repeat	smile	table	twenty	why
return	snow	take	twice	wife
rice	so	talk	two	will
rich	soap	tall	type	winter
right	some	tea		with
river	somebody	teach		woman
road	somehow	telephone	umbrella	(women)
room	someone	tell	uncle	word
round	something	ten	understand	work
run	sometimes	test	university	would
	somewhere	thank	up	write
	son	the	us	wrong
sad	song	their	use	
salt	soon	them		
same	sorry	themselves		year
say	soup	then	very	yellow
school	south	therefore		yes
second	speak	these		yesterday
see	spell	they	wait	you
sell	spend	thin	wake	young
send	spoon	thing	walk	your
seven	sport	think	wall	yourself
she	spring	third	want	yourselves

In addition, the following closed sets have been assumed:

days of the week
months of the year
cardinal numbers
ordinal numbers

Words in Volume 1

Numbers refer to **volume** and unit.

accept, **1**-1
address, **1**-6
advantage, **1**-12
afternoon, **1**-15
air force, **1**-18
airplane, **1**-2
airport, **1**-2
allow, **1**-8
ambition, **1**-14
ambulance, **1**-16
apartment, **1**-3
apply, **1**-1
army, **1**-18
around, **1**-19
artist, **1**-14
assign(ment), **1**-8
attempt, **1**-1
audience, **1**-9
automobile, **1**-2

back, **1**-16
bacon, **1**-15
band, **1**-25
barn, **1**-19
baseball, **1**-10
basement, **1**-12
beach, **1**-9
beef, **1**-15
bell, **1**-8

bench, **1**-9
bicycle, **1**-11
bill, **1**-24
bleed/blood, **1**-16
blow, **1**-4
body, **1**-16
boot, **1**-17
boring, **1**-9
boss, **1**-5
bowl, **1**-15
break, **1**-16
brick, **1**-12
bridge, **1**-11
bus, **1**-2
business, **1**-5

cafeteria, **1**-8
camera, **1**-7
camp, **1**-21
campus, **1**-8
card, **1**-21
careful/less, **1**-5
carry, **1**-7
cave, **1**-21
cent, **1**-6
chair, **1**-12
change, **1**-17
chapter, **1**-8
cheap, **1**-6

cheese, **1**-15
choose, **1**-8
clear, **1**-4
clerk, **1**-6
climb, **1**-21
coast, **1**-23
collect (call), **1**-24
college, **1**-1
comedy, **1**-25
comfortable, **1**-12
commit, **1**-22
common, **1**-16
communicate, **1**-6
company, **1**-5
compete, **1**-10
complete, **1**-1
concert, **1**-9
contract, **1**-14
cool, **1**-21
corn, **1**-19
cost, **1**-21
course, **1**-8
crime, **1**-22
cross, **1**-11
crowd, **1**-10

date, **1**-21
decide, **1**-3
declare, **1**-20

Words in Volume 2

Numbers refer to **volume** and unit.

APPENDIX
E

Words in Volume 3

Numbers refer to **volume** and unit.

abbreviation, **3**-5
about, **3**-7
abrupt, **3**-5
academic, **3**-23
accomplish, **3**-2
accurate, **3**-13
accustomed to, **3**-8
achieve, **3**-23
acid, **3**-10
action, **3**-9
activity, **3**-12
admire, **3**-21
admit, **3**-1
adult, **3**-14
adventure, **3**-20
afford, **3**-8
afterward, **3**-15
against, **3**-9
agree(ment), **3**-18
airmail, **3**-5
alert, **3**-9
alive, **3**-19
almost, **3**-1
aloud, **3**-22
alter, **3**-4
although, **3**-14
altitude, **3**-8
amateur, **3**-21
amount, **3**-15
and, **3**-11

anger, **3**-14
ankle, **3**-19
announce, **3**-24
apology, **3**-18
appear(ance), **3**-4
appetite, **3**-15
approve (of), **3**-14
argue, **3**-2
assign, **3**-24
at once, **3**-2
athletic, **3**-23
atmosphere, **3**-10
attached, **3**-16
attend, **3**-22
attention (pay), **3**-1
attitude, **3**-7
average, **3**-1

backwards, **3**-3
balloon, **3**-12
bar, **3**-21
based on (basis), **3**-7
battle, **3**-20
beard, **3**-14
bee, **3**-12
beer, **3**-15
beg, **3**-9
behave, **3**-14
behind, **3**-23

belong to, **3**-14
below, **3**-6
bet, **3**-21
biography, **3**-7
birth, **3**-19
bite, **3**-17
blame, **3**-9
blank, **3**-13
blond, **3**-14
bother, **3**-9
bottle, **3**-15
bottom, **3**-6
brain, **3**-19
brave, **3**-20
bride, **3**-14
budget, **3**-18
burn, **3**-15
burst, **3**-12
bury, **3**-22
butter, **3**-15

cage, **3**-17
calculate, **3**-23
calm, **3**-17
candidate, **3**-18
candle, **3**-22
candy, **3**-15
captain, **3**-20
capture, **3**-20

Index

Words in Volume 4

Numbers refer to **volume** and unit.